You Don't Need Nipples to Get Into Heaven...

CHRIS WEAVER

11/07

Join me as we
"Draw near with
confidence!"

Chris Weaver
Hebrews 4:16

xulon PRESS

Dedication

For my treasured life-long girlfriend, Stan,
and for the myriads of
other breast cancer survivors,

and for those of you who are currently forging
the courageous fight against this terrible disease.

Take courage; draw strength; PRESS ON and fight, fight, fight!
At this very moment He's upholding you with
His righteous right hand.

"Fear not, for I am with you; be not dismayed, for I am your God.
I will strengthen you, yes, I will help you, I will uphold you with
My righteous right hand." (Isaiah 41:10 NKJV)

Acknowledgment

First and foremost, I want to publicly profess my abiding faith in Jesus Christ. There are no words to express the vastness of His mercy and faithfulness, or to express my profound gratitude to Him.

Nor are there words to describe the indescribable love, comfort and support I draw from my husband, Bill, our daughters Sarah and Amy and from my parents, Helen and George.

My thoughts are also with all of you who have continuously encouraged me to write this book. I want to especially acknowledge Tom Grady who was the first to approach me on the subject, and Dean Moore who was the catalyst God used to inspire me to finally begin the writing process...nearly twenty years after Tom planted the seed.

To my doctors and nurses and medical staff who each cared for me with such tenderness I felt the Master's very touch through them.

Thank you all from the depths of my heart and soul. May you receive as abundantly as you have given.

"I thank my God in all my remembrance of you." (Philippians 1:3[NASB])

Contents

Preface

This book was written on my heart long before it ever reached the page. I held it deep within me for years, not wanting to revisit these extraordinarily personal and gruelingly emotional events. Yet I always knew that one day I would set free what I had locked deep within me.

With all of my heart I know Jesus allowed me the privilege of this experience...yes, the PRIVILEGE...so He would receive glory and so others would draw strength and encouragement from Him. That is my driving passion. That is why I have, at long last, obeyed His tug on my heart and written this book.

I am certainly no breast cancer expert. I am simply a woman who has embarked upon the journey and whose commitment to encourage fellow-journeywomen is unyielding.

I believe that somewhere another woman, perhaps even this very day, may be facing what I faced. I want to scream from the rooftops that GOD IS FAITHFUL! I want her to KNOW He is. Although this is my story, the message is about HIM! I may have taken the journey, but Jesus Christ directed each step.

So, if you're frightened by the "dreaded diagnosis"...or frightened by even the *possibility* of getting the "dreaded diagnosis," this book is written for you! I implore you to take a deep breath...and then take the first step on your journey. He has set the path before you and will never leave you or forsake you.

My precious sister, take heart...place your trust and hope in Him. He is FAITHFUL.

CHAPTER ONE

ॐ

The Astronauts Have Nothing on Spice

It was just another Saturday morning, different only in the fact that my husband was giving me the extraordinary treat of a few additional moments to spend in bed as he tended to our two young daughters, Sarah and Amy. I remember pulling the comforter up snugly under my chin and looking up at the sunbeams flickering across our bedroom ceiling. I listened to Bill and the girls downstairs in the kitchen making breakfast together. What a great moment. Our cat, Spice, couldn't resist joining me and jumped up onto the bed stepping carefully over the folds in the blankets searching for the perfect place to settle down. As he stepped onto my leg and then up over my stomach, he couldn't possibly know that his next step would change all of our lives forever.

Spice nearly became the first cat launched into orbit right from the comfort of his very own home! I could see the headlines now, "Cat Thrust Through Bedroom Ceiling Lands on Moon, full story on page eleven." Spice just missed becoming the first cat in the space program, but

I was the one who literally "saw stars." In his quest for the ideal cuddling spot, our much-loved cat had accidentally stepped onto my chest and apparently right onto a tumor. Pain surged through my body and in one swift move I flipped poor Spice up into the air as I thrashed in the bed; my head spinning. What in the world just happened? I'm sure Spice was asking himself the same question.

So much for lazing in the bed!

I think I knew in that flash of a fraction of a miniscule moment that I was in trouble. Something inside me just knew it. I think God gives us that special insight. As I look back now, I truly believe He prepared me then and there for the arduous journey ahead.

Incredibly, I was not engulfed in fear, although I was certainly stunned. I wouldn't say that I was in denial, nor would I say that I was unsuspecting. I had a keen awareness of the situation, yet I can't explain precisely what I was feeling. I do know that for some strange reason I did not tell Bill what had just happened.

❦✻❦

CHAPTER TWO

Merrily We Roll Along

It was the mid-eighties. Ann Jillian…Shirley Temple Black…Betty Ford…a cousin…my grandmother…that was about the extent of my awareness of breast cancer.

Sure, during routine gynecological exams I had been told that because I had full, dense breasts it was more difficult for the doctor to detect breast lumps by physical examination alone. So, I underwent a mammogram. Ten years earlier, when I was in my late twenties, I had even had breast surgery to remove a "mass" which turned out to be a benign fibroid adenoma. Actually, I had nine benign fibroid adenomas removed in three separate surgical procedures over that ten-year period.

I had numerous follow-up exams, x-rays, more mammograms, more check-ups and, of course, performed self-examinations.

I had nursed both Sarah and Amy for the benefit of their health and nutrition, but also because I had read somewhere in the reams of pre-natal literature new mothers devour, that nursing also promoted breast health. All in all, I thought I was taking pretty good care of myself.

Perhaps that's why I was so cavalier about Spice's discovery. I just filed it away and went merrily rolling along…

…until I felt the lump again.

I could feel it INTERNALLY...pressing downward underneath my breast, pushing low into my chest cavity. I couldn't feel it with my fingers; I felt the result of the pressure of my fingers.

I did mention something about this to Bill at some point. You would think this conversation would be one we would never forget, but the truth is neither Bill nor I can recall it specifically. Bill tried to feel for the mass, but he could not detect anything. Still, I knew I felt something hard, pressing downward, inside my body. I knew it.

Because all of my previous "masses" had been benign, we wanted to believe there was nothing to be alarmed about this time. Somewhere in the back of my mind, however, a seed of concern began to germinate. Again, I know now that was my heavenly Father's doing.

I began to more frequently perform breast self-examination and during a regular check-up, I mentioned Spice's discovery to my gynecologist, a fine Christian man who also happened to be a member of our church. I scheduled an office visit during which he diligently tried to find whatever it was that I was feeling. He told me that my breasts were not only dense; they also contained massive scar tissue resulting from my previous procedures. That combination made mere physical detection of a mass nearly impossible. Further complicating the situation, I had had twenty-one mammograms by then, exposing me to higher than normal amounts of cancer-causing radiation and he was hesitant to expose me to even more.

This was yet another complexity and my tiny seed of concern began to sprout roots. I felt like I was a bit between a rock and a hard place...no one could feel the lump I knew was there and further mammograms were not a viable option for me.

My doctor ordered an ultrasound examination, which is designed to detect areas of thickening in breast tissue possibly indicating the presence of a tumor. It is not as pictorially clear as mammography, but it is helpful in some situations. The results of my ultrasound indicated several areas of thickening in my breast tissue. Unfortunately, there was really no way of knowing if this was just my scar tissue or a more serious problem. I was in a potentially dangerous situation.

For the first time, my doctor mentioned the option of mastectomy and suggested I see a breast specialist.

Oh, dear. A fruit-bearing plant of fear was now growing in my mind. Bill and I began to pray with greater intensity.

꘎

CHAPTER THREE

Here's a Nice One, Bill

Bill's prayers and support and love and concern and level-headed perseverance literally sustained me. The details of that time in my life still make me a bit woozy.

It was Bill who suggested we meet together with my gynecologist one last time before seeing the breast specialist. We definitely felt more comfortable discussing options with someone we both knew and trusted. We needed more details, more information and he was wonderfully understanding and more than happy to meet with us in his office.

He clearly and professionally explained the situation in further detail, but Bill was the only one who was actually listening to the doctor. I saw their lips moving; I heard the sound of their conversation, but I just sat in the chair mentally tending to the virtual garden of concern that was now growing. I was becoming quite the little farmer!

When I heard the words "mastectomy" and "reconstruction" I finally forced myself to tune in. Just in the nick of time, I might add. Out of a file drawer comes a dandy little medical catalogue of breasts. Actually, they were reconstructive breast implants. With great clinical enthusiasm, my doctor actually pointed to some breast forms on the page and said to my HUSBAND, "Bill, this is a very popular model. How do you like these?" I couldn't believe it! Poor Bill didn't know what to say. I felt like shouting, "Hey, what about ME? I'm the one, after all, who would be sporting those beauties, shouldn't I be the one to pick 'em out?" I find it so amusing that God enables us to find humor in our circumstances…even difficult ones!

CHAPTER FOUR

Never Again

And these were certainly difficult times. My symptoms now also included an unusual discharge and I could tell the mass was getting larger. We knew it was time to see the breast specialist. I made an appointment with the recommended doctor, and when the day of the visit finally arrived Bill arranged to take the day off work so he could be with me. We were in this together and he knew I needed him there.

Bill and I sat and sat and sat in the waiting room. Hour after hour went by. Yes, HOURS went by and we still sat. And so did many other frustrated and upset women. It had taken weeks to get the appointment, and now I still had to wait to see the doctor. Waiting is torture.

Finally, I was called back into an examination room. The nurse took me back first so I could change into that lovely little paper ensemble and then Bill would join me. Or so I thought.

Now I was waiting again…in the freezing cold examination room, propped on the table, garbed in the little paper gown. No magazine. No Bill. No nurse. No doctor. My mind racing. Finally, at long last, the doctor arrived.

"Hello, Mrs. (pause) as he looks at the chart for my name, Mrs. Weaver."

"Doctor, my husband is in the waiting room, he's taken the day off work, he wants to hear this," I managed to say. Sorry, Charlie. No time to get Bill. He proceeded full-speed ahead. Without Bill.

I explained to the breast specialist the details of my current situation, my history of breast lumps, the scar tissue, the mammograms, the lump I could feel, the discharge, the symptoms and the whole scenario.

He felt no mass.

Not surprised, I told him that my gynecologist mentioned mastectomy for this very reason.

"Why do you want a mastectomy?" he barked sternly.

"I don't WANT a mastectomy. I am afraid I could have undetected breast cancer." There, I said it. I had finally verbalized my greatest fear.

"So you want to cut off your breast in case you have cancer. What are you going to do next; cut out your liver because you're afraid you might have liver cancer, too?

Get dressed." (His voice now laced with disgust.)

With that the doctor, the highly recommended breast specialist, was gone. I sat there in silence. In absolute shock.

That is the honest truth of what happened and what was said to me that day.

I carried my paperwork to the reception desk as the nurse told me I needed a follow-up appointment. For some reason, unbelievably, I made a follow-up appointment with this doctor.

Four weeks later, Bill again took the day off work to go to the appointment with me.

When we arrived at the medical complex that morning, we remained in our parked car and we prayed. We needed God's wisdom, His direction. His peace.

Again, we waited for hours to see the specialist. (We later learned that appointments were routinely triple-booked, hence the lengthy waits.)

I was summoned and led to the examination room. Again, no Bill. I was absolutely astounded by the disregard for Bill's time and utter dismissal of my need for Bill's presence. I silently prayed that God would help me to remain calm, to assuage my trepidations, to present concise questions and to be alert to the doctor's response. I prayed for my doctor to thoroughly examine my breast and clearly detect the mass I knew was present within my body.

Again, this is an exact description of what happened:

The doctor entered the examination room and began to palpate my breast. I heard him say something and as I was about to ask him some of my gut-wrenching questions, I saw that he had a headphone and mouthpiece attached to his head and I immediately realized he was talking on the telephone as he was conducting his examination. He wasn't even speaking to me; he was in the midst of a conversation with someone else. I actually heard him whispering about what he wanted for dinner that evening! There was no possible way for him to hear my questions, let alone address them. How could he possibly be concentrating on finding the lump in my breast? Was this really happening? I was livid. And I was really frightened. I desperately needed a doctor. I needed his expertise and his help. I felt a lump. I had a discharge. I might have cancer. What was going on?

After completing his incredibly brief assessment, and with no interaction between us, the doctor exited the room as mysteriously as he had appeared. I dressed and made my way to the receptionist's desk with paperwork in hand and unresolved concerns in mind. She glanced at the papers and told me the doctor had once again indicated he wanted to see me in another month. This time I had the courage to inform her in no uncertain terms that there was absolutely no way I would ever see this doctor again. I didn't care if he was the last breast specialist on earth. And I meant it. (In my mind I heard a supportive standing ovation resounding from the women still corralled in the stagnant waiting area.)

I called my gynecologist to notify him of my distressing experience with the breast specialist. He listened very intently, and thanked me for the information. I knew he was sincere.

I have since learned from other women that this specialist also treated them in a similarly disrespectful and unprofessional way. In my opinion, that was clearly malpractice. I do not know if he is still in practice today.

Eventually, with the help of the Holy Spirit, my spiritual eyes were opened. I realized I had been so preoccupied and trapped in the poisonous mire of self-pity, anger and bitterness I had lost my focus on God's Divine providence in answered prayer. Bill and I had prayed for God's direction, and through these trying circumstances, He *was* directing us. He may have closed this door, but others would open. I was looking only at the present circumstances and, therefore, could see nothing but frustration and fear. He is at work in our lives whether we "see" it or not. That's the very essence of faith. I humbly asked God's forgiveness of my response.

Jesus performed a miraculous work in my heart, and I learned one more valuable lesson in trust for which I am truly grateful.

In time I was able to forgive the breast specialist as well. I was attending a women's retreat and during one particular session the minister focused the lesson on forgiveness. At the end of his lecture we were asked to prayerfully search our hearts to determine if there was someone we needed to forgive. Jesus knew there was still some "business" for me to take care of and He brought that doctor to my mind. The speaker then told us that he would be available to "stand in" for anyone we needed to forgive and instructed us that we could step forward right then and privately and prayerfully do so. One by one various women took advantage of this generous opportunity and many lives were set free. As I witnessed this, I experienced the pounding heartbeat and gripping knot in my stomach that always meant God was prompting me to action.

I made my way to the "stand in" and explained that he represented a doctor who very nearly cost me my life. Out it all poured. "Doctor, you didn't LISTEN to me. You didn't take me seriously. You didn't respect me and you didn't respect Bill. I felt alone. I needed your HELP and you mocked me..." I was literally shaking as the "stand-in" doctor waited for me to profess it all.

Then, quietly, he said, "Please forgive me. I didn't know Jesus personally; I was doing the best I could for you..." I think he said some other things also, but I don't recall the specifics. I heard all I needed to hear, all Jesus intended for me to hear. Suddenly I was filled with compassion for the doctor.

He didn't know Jesus. There was no way he could have given me what I needed at the time. Jesus knew that. I was still in HIS protective arms, still being upheld by His righteous right hand; still completely safe, no matter who my doctor was at the time. Tears flowed as I humbly asked the "stand-in" doctor to forgive me for all the anger

I had been harboring against him for so long. I asked forgiveness for only seeing things from my perspective and never attempting to extend compassion or grace to him. I forgave the breast specialist via the "stand-in" and the burden of unforgiveness was lifted and I, too, was set free from the encumbrance forevermore. I felt like dancing!

"For if you forgive men for their transgressions, your heavenly Father will also forgive you." (Matthew 6:14 NASB)

It is still my prayer, however, that doctors and nurses and lab technicians and receptionists would see beyond the routine of their day-to-day activities and realize that the patients they are treating, as well as their family members, face some of the most difficult challenges imaginable. We need empathy and sensitivity and respect. We need you to make the phone call on Friday instead of putting it off until Monday. We're waiting by the phone all weekend for those results.

Meanwhile, I had a major problem and a breast specialist I did not trust to treat it.

CHAPTER FIVE

Look At My Eyes

As a result of the distressing ordeal with the breast specialist, I did not have the physical or emotional strength to visit any more doctors. My symptoms persisted and I couldn't deny or stop thinking about what was going on inside my body, yet I took no tangible action. Months and months went by. Understandable, perhaps, but not exactly rational thinking to be sure! I was sinking into fear and hopelessness. With love and compassion, Jesus mercifully intervened once again and directed my path in spite of my reluctance to act.

Breast cancer awareness began to increase and great strides were being made in research and treatments. I couldn't pick up a magazine without seeing an article about a new study. There was an information surge in the news and on television. The pink ribbons started to appear. More and more was being discovered about breast health and breast cancer prevention. Women were speaking more openly about their personal battles with breast cancer solely for the benefit of others. It was amazing.

Yet, I was still paralyzed, wanting to put my own situation out of my mind and just move on, just forget about it. But I couldn't. Breasts. Breasts. Breasts. Morning, noon and night. It seemed that was all I ever heard about!

Deep down, I knew God was directing me to get help, but I really didn't know where to turn. So He sent me my own personal angel. His messenger. Her name is Kitty.

Kitty and I had become great friends through our church. We served side-by-side on the women's ministry team, attended the weekly Bible study as well as many other church activities.

Our husbands served together on various committees as well. We all socialized together, and our children were friends.

Kitty and I talked and laughed and enjoyed one another. We spoke on the phone. We discussed current events. We shared recipes. We were women, we were friends. We loved and respected one another.

Kitty is one of the best mothers I have ever known. I admire her greatly and have learned so much from her. She had an absolutely amazing way of getting the undivided attention of her three sons. She would gently admonish them saying, "Look at my eyes." That was her "code" and they knew instantly that she had something important to say and they'd better listen up!

One day I happened to mention my growing concern over the fact that I could still feel the lump that nobody else seemed able to feel. I told Kitty about an article I had recently read in a magazine. The article contained a telephone number that enabled you to speak personally, live, with a breast cancer survivor at any time, twenty-four hours a day. One day I called the number. I poured my heart out to an absolute stranger in a state on the other side of the country. She completely understood what I was going through. She told me, and I will never forget her words, "Women know their own bodies better than anyone. If you feel a lump, get yourself to a doctor who will LISTEN to you!" Her words pierced my heart.

I told Kitty what the woman had said to me and that's all Kitty needed to hear. She didn't miss a beat. "So, when are you going to call a doctor?" She knew I was too frightened to make the call.

I promise you that Kitty called me every single day to ask if I had made a doctor's appointment yet.

"No, not yet, Kitty."

Ring-Ring.
Ring-Ring.
Ring-Ring.

No kidding. Every single day.

Kitty would NOT let this slide. She demonstrated God's steadfastness. She was devoted to me, just as my heavenly Father is, and I knew she was being used as His instrument in my life.

One Friday Kitty had had quite enough of my absurd excuses. She gave me an ultimatum. No more procrastination. Yup. In the midst of her ultimatum, right over the telephone, she pulled no punches and uttered the power-packed words, "Chris, look at my eyes." I listened up, just as her sons always did. "Either you make an appointment today or I am going to make it for you." I knew Kitty was serious. And I knew I had to face what I was avoiding.

I hung up the phone and dialed the number of a doctor Kitty had gotten the name of. Kitty didn't know the doctor personally, but she knew someone who had gone to him. His office was located on the opposite side of the large city we lived in, about forty-five minutes away from my home.

At that point, it simply didn't matter where the doctor was located. Kitty was on the move and I'd better just make the appointment.

So on that Friday morning I called the doctor's office, explained my situation and, amazingly, got an immediate appointment. On Monday afternoon I saw the doctor.

CHAPTER SIX

What an Aura

Bill and I had prayed all weekend for God's absolute direction. We asked that He guide us with a specific course of action and give us specific answers, through this third new doctor, to the many frightening questions we still faced.

I decided to go to this appointment alone. In the waiting room I had been so busy praying, reviewing my questions and completing the necessary forms that I hadn't even noticed that the only other patient waiting to be seen by the doctor was a middle-aged *man* with an enormous bandage on his NOSE!

"Now, what?" I thought to myself. "What in the world am I doing here? What kind of doctor am I about to see?" I tried to remember who Kitty had said referred this doctor to her. Maybe I'd better check into this a little more…

Too late. It was my turn. Off I trotted to the examination room, following behind the nurse like a baby duck. As we made our way down the hall, I seized the moment and asked exactly what type of doctor I was about to see. I was getting nervous.

The nurse explained that the doctor is a surgeon. Surgeon???? Oh, dear, I'm definitely in the wrong place! With me already up on the paper-lined examination table, she began taking my history. "Where do you feel the lump, Mrs. Weaver?" I showed her and, like all the others, she was not able to feel anything. Once again, I explained that I felt it pushing down into my body, not up from my body.

Incredibly, she said, "I know just what you are talking about." The nurse went on to tell me that she herself had just returned to work after undergoing breast surgery. To my absolute shock, she then unbuttoned the front of her uniform to proudly and courageously show me her post-surgical body. She was saying other encouraging things, but honestly I remember her kind, calm, reassuring tone of voice more than her words. As shocked as I was by her little "peep" show, I will never forget her selflessness in doing it.

Still, this was one strange experience.

The doctor's examination was clinical and professional and, like those before him, he stated that no specific lumps were detected. After dressing, I was to meet with him in his office. This was getting to be too much for me.

The furniture in the doctor's office was arranged in such a way that it was necessary to walk past his desk in order to sit in the patient's chair facing the doctor. In other words, the entrance and exit from his office was behind him.

I sat in my chair, still trying to compose myself. "Mrs. Weaver," the doctor said, "With your secondary-familial involvement, your prolonged uninterrupted exposure to estrogen, your breast history, your vast scar tissue and dense breasts, your excessive amounts of radiation exposure due to mammography, your inconclusive sonograms, with your previous breast involvement and your current presentation of symptoms, it is my opinion that you have absolutely no choice other than mastectomy. Yours is a unique combination of complications which place you in a dangerous position of great risk."

I didn't immediately respond. I think I may have even smiled, not at the grave news, but at the fact that at long last this doctor had just answered our prayers. He presented the facts in no uncertain terms and I was grateful beyond measure.

I think I even thanked him. He asked me a few more questions and we discussed my current symptoms. In the midst of our discussion the doctor suddenly leaned back in his chair, looked right at me and said, "Mrs. Weaver, you have an actual aura about you," and he made a waving motion with his arms as he continued to look at me.

I must admit that freaked me out a little. Is this guy for real? Is he some "new-age" guru? I literally grabbed for my purse and was going to bolt from his office, when I realized I would have to walk right past him in order to leave. It was impossible to make a clean get-away! It was then that I had an absolute awareness that God, in His foresight, had even known that because of the doctor's furniture arrangement, I had no choice but to stay put in my chair and listen to the doctor. So I stayed put. I knew that Jesus had taken care of every single detail. I was filled with God's peace. I knew I was precisely where I needed to be.

The doctor continued the discussion and went on to say that when women face surgery of this magnitude, they often have quite emotional reactions to the prospect of mastectomy. He told me that he sees women EVERY day who choose DEATH over mastectomy. Apparently they can't deal with the loss and they equate their value as women with their breasts. Sadly, I'm sure our society's obsessive emphasis on breasts reinforces this concept.

My reaction, the doctor said, was atypical. I told him that I considered the surgery to be the *solution* to my problem, not the problem itself.

In the midst of our conversation, the doctor picked up his phone and dialed a number. Again, not knowing exactly what to expect, I just sat there. "Hello, doctor." (He was speaking with another doctor, describing my situation in very technical medical terminology that I didn't understand and don't remember.) Looking directly at me, the doctor went on to say, "No, she is very calm. She has a definite aura about her. Okay. Wednesday morning. Great. Thank you. Bye."

(The aura again. To this day, I don't know if he actually SAW something, but apparently he was impressed by the fact that I was at such peace.)

After hanging up the phone, he explained to me that because mastectomy is a highly specialized surgery, he had referred me to another surgeon whom I was to meet with on that Wednesday morning. He had made all the arrangements for me.

And that was that. I never saw this doctor or his nurse or the man with the bandaged nose again. But there is absolutely no doubt in my mind that they were personal gifts to me from my Heavenly Father. They were without a doubt answers to our prayers and I was in awe of our almighty, yet personal, intimate, deeply caring God.

CHAPTER SEVEN

The "Philosophy"

On Wednesday morning, I headed out to meet with the fourth doctor. This time I went rather blindly, having been referred by the previous doctor whom I really didn't know either. At this point, I just stopped asking and went.

The waiting room was neat and tidy, decorated in soothing pastel colors and the furniture was upholstered beautifully. There were fresh flowers on the side tables.

I went up to the check-in window and was greeted by a friendly woman sporting a big smile. "Oh, hello Mrs. Weaver. We have been waiting for you." Waiting for me!? Then the DOCTOR came out and greeted me in the reception room and the DOCTOR escorted me back to his office, not an examination room. The DOCTOR offered me something to drink. The DOCTOR took my coat. The DOCTOR seated me. It was unbelievable.

In a gentle, very caring yet totally professional manner, the doctor took my history. He listened as if my words were of vital importance to him. He questioned and reviewed and questioned again. Then he led me into the examination room where he introduced me to his nurse as he left the room.

She gave me a soft, CLOTH gown and instructed me to change into the gown behind the privacy screen which was in the corner of the room, then sit on the table and just let them know when I was emotionally ready to be seen. Was I dreaming?

The doctor and nurse entered and he began the physical examination. Very thorough examination; same conclusion. He suggested I return in a month so he could "track my breasts."

I couldn't wait to tell Bill how unusual this experience had been. I described how incredible the doctor was. How respectful of me. How devoted his staff was. They made a definite impression on me.

One day the receptionist called and asked if I could come to the office before my follow-up appointment in order to complete some additional insurance paperwork. Bill owned his own graphic design business and medical insurance for the self-employed was extremely expensive. Our policy was very limited in coverage, but the most cost-effective for us at the time. I went to the doctor's office and when I arrived, the receptionist and I were alone in the office. The doctor and nurse were in surgery so there were no other patients waiting either. I chatted with the receptionist as I filled out one form after another.

I told her that I had never seen a more caring doctor and how impressed I was by his kindness. "Oh yes, he lives by a certain philosophy." She then said, "We all have that philosophy or the doctor wouldn't want us to work here." Oh, oh. I hope she doesn't say anything about an aura! I decided I'd better find out precisely what "philosophy" she was talking about. So I asked her point blank. Her answer floored me. "We are all CHRISTIANS," she replied. "We have been praying for you, Mrs. Weaver. We believe God brought you to us."

Her words live in my heart. I will never, ever forget them. I managed to say, "I am a Christian also." I could not contain my tears. I rambled on about how we had also prayed and prayed. I remember her knowing smile. She told me that both she and the nurse had also undergone mastectomies and understood exactly what I was going through so they knew just how to pray for me.

She told me the doctor's wife also worked in the office as an accountant/insurance liaison. She was praying for me as well. The receptionist went on to tell me that my doctor had been a pathologist for twenty years prior to his becoming a surgeon. And not only was he a surgeon, he was a plastic and reconstructive surgeon specializing in breast health. He had devoted his entire career to helping women.

I knew, beyond any doubt whatsoever, that my loving God had His very hand upon me. The personal confirmation was absolutely overwhelming. I have never felt safer; more secure; more fearless. Whatever my future held, I knew my steps were being directed by the One Who knew me best. Only God could have orchestrated my incredible journey to the doctor of HIS choice, this fourth-generation referral.

I stand, I stand in awe of You.
Holy God, for Who all praise is due.
I stand in awe of You.

CHAPTER EIGHT

Getting to Know You

I went for my follow-up visit and a few subsequent follow-ups. The doctor said he was "getting to know my breasts." That was his actual terminology. He was looking for any changes, which he did discover. My symptoms now also included some external skin puckering.

On each visit he took photographs depicting my body from neck to torso. You get the idea. It was terribly uncomfortable. My doctor showed me his files of "before and after" photos of other "brave women" as he called them, who have also undergone this procedure. I looked at pages of anonymous women's "before" and "after" breasts. The experience was surreal.

In an effort to be extra thorough, my doctor ordered one more mammogram. He also asked my permission to present my case at an International Breast Symposium which was being held in our city. Renowned breast specialists from around the world would gather to study and discuss my unique case. Complete with photos. I could just imagine them projected in living color on the enormous overhead screen.

The international breast specialists unanimously confirmed mastectomy as my only option. It was time to take action.

Bill and I met with my doctor in his office. He prayed as our meeting began. The doctor told us he recommended prophylactic bi-lateral subcutaneous mastectomies with immediate reconstruction utilizing silicone breast implants. I was okay with the mastectomies, but very reluctant to have the reconstruction. I remembered reading as a teenager about the horrible complications women suffered after having silicone injections. The doctor assured me that the implants he used were made of silicone gel, contained in a silicone casing and wrapped in a silicone mesh, which prevented breast implant "hardening." He gave me several articles to read. He apprised me of the great improvements that had been made over the years. He showed me photographs of what a woman's chest looked like post-mastectomy, with no reconstruction. It was pretty unsettling.

The doctor presented the other reconstruction options also. The saline injections, the pedicle flap, and the tram flap (transverse rectus abdominis muscle flap) in which my own muscle and fat cells could be harvested to construct a breast made of my own tissue. A "tummy tuck" would be an added bonus with a tram flap. It is, however, a much more complicated procedure with a longer period of recovery. He gave me a stack of literature to read detailing all of the reconstruction options, and left the decision totally up to me. I appreciated that so much. I needed to feel some sort of control over the grim situation that controlled me.

After much prayer and discussion, Bill and I decided to proceed with the bi-lateral surgery and immediate reconstruction utilizing the silicone breast implants. Again, the doctor asked to meet with us in person. This time he asked that Sarah and Amy join us as well.

Sarah was nine years old, and Amy seven. We had explained the situation to them in terms we believed they could understand. Even at their young ages they knew full well that something serious was going on. The doctor, who had eight children of his own, suggested the girls come so they could ask him any questions they may have when we met. Is that not a caring man?

Sarah asked if her breasts were going to be "chopped off" when she grew up. The doctor had sample implants displayed on his desk and Amy asked if she could touch them. He was very patient and looked right at the girls and spoke directly to them as he answered all their questions. He understood they needed to be included in this process and the girls liked him very much. Bill and the girls were excused to the waiting room as the doctor had one more exercise for me.

He wanted to show me that I didn't have to fear living normally with breast implants. He wanted to demonstrate how strong they are so he POUNDED them with all his might. I kid you not, he made a fist and gave those babies a big ole' punch with all of his strength! I know I gasped. Then he flung them onto the floor and JUMPED and STOMPED on them! He said they would not rupture even if a seat belt suddenly sprung into action. He did warn me that the only thing to avoid was wearing pins…decorative pins, pins used in some name tags or to secure corsages, etc. Pins could penetrate the protective shell and actually puncture the implant. Barring that event, he told me they came with a "lifetime guarantee" and that when my body was old and wrinkled and laid out in my coffin, my breasts would look young and perky and as good as new! Great, doc, box 'em up, I'll take a pair.

Too bad it wasn't that simple. But I got the point, and his graphic demonstration definitely did accomplish its purpose. I had no residual fear of the implants. I was fully in the "go" mode for reconstruction and by then was more than ready to have the mastectomies. Finally, nearly eight months after Spice's discovery, the surgery was scheduled to take place in a week and a half. That was fine with me; I wanted the problem mass removed from my breast as soon as possible. I knew there was a time bomb tick-tick-ticking within my body.

CHAPTER NINE

Not So Fast There, Lady

By now word of the situation had spread, and we truly had no idea how many people were lifting us up in prayer. Our pastor and the members of our church, members of the women's Bible Studies I attended, Bill's men's group, family members, friends, prayer chains, the headmaster, school board members, teaching staff and even students at the Christian school our girls attended. It was humbling, but so very reassuring. I found myself more and more unable to pray myself and I took great comfort in the fact that others were interceding on our behalf. Actually, I depended on it.

For some reason, I was led to ask my friend Penny to pray for me as I underwent the final pre-op mammogram my doctor had ordered. It was unusual for me to make such a request. I was not nervous for by now mammograms had certainly become a familiar exercise. I was not sure what prompted my asking Penny to pray for this one remaining exam, but before long I came to understand why.

For the most part this mammogram was as routine as all the others I had had, except for the fact that the radiologist read my films immediately and asked to see me before I left to go home. After dressing, I met with the radiologist in his office. I had never met with a radiologist before. The test results were always sent on to my doctor who gave me the report. This was a definite departure from standard procedure and I was a bit shaken.

The radiologist wanted to confirm that I was scheduled for bi-lateral mastectomies. "Yes, that is correct," I said. He then proceeded to inform me that he saw absolutely no reason for such a radical procedure. There was no unusual indication of breast mass or "thickening" on my films. He was quite animated, almost angry. He told me I should reconsider having surgery.

After everything I had been through up to this point, I was completely taken aback by his statements at the eleventh hour. I could feel myself getting more and more upset. I kept silently repeating to myself, "Confusion is not of the Lord." I think I said something to the doctor about a mass in my left breast that I could actually feel. The radiologist did not back off. I believe he had good intentions and without the benefit of knowing all of my history and unusual risk factors, he was just trying to preserve my breasts. Unfortunately, he sent me reeling into a downward spiral of fear and concern.

I called Penny as soon as I got home. I was crying as I tried to describe the morning's bizarre events. Penny prayed with me over the phone and reassured me that

I should just stay the course. Her words were calm, but powerful. She exhorted me to realize that this was not just a battle for my physical health; this was Spiritual warfare! She reminded me that, above all, God is in control. She encouraged me to keep my eyes firmly fixed on Jesus.

Intercessory prayer is one of the most significant gifts we can give one another. We are challenged to *pray one for another*" in James 5:16 and the sacrifice of prayer tangibly demonstrates our love for one another.

Bill and I drew upon the strength of intercessory prayer as we faced the next major obstacle.

CHAPTER TEN

This Calls for a Toast!

Living in limbo had been mental anguish. I can't describe how relieved I was feeling to finally have a course of action at long last. The seemingly endless ordeal was about to be over. That is truly the way I viewed it. I was actually looking forward to my surgery. Perhaps that seems strange, but I had felt so totally vulnerable for so long and just helpless with no way of detecting potential disaster, that I had become completely exhausted emotionally. I was ready to face whatever the doctor discovered as a result of my surgery. More than ready.

My cat Spice had the sensation of flying in outer space. I now discovered what the astronauts must feel when their mission gets scrubbed at the last minute. I was on the launching pad of my operation, and my mission was scrubbed.

Unbelievably, I received a phone call from my doctor's office just days before my surgery was to take place. Our insurance company would not approve my procedure.

The hospital put on the brakes. "Lord, what is going on?" I whispered under my breath.

After numerous phone calls, floods of paperwork and even a personal phone call from my doctor to our insurance company, Bill finally resolved the dilemma. He made the decision to proceed with or without pre-approval from our insurance company. God had led us this far and He would provide what we needed either through our insurance company or in a way known only to Him. We would step out in faith. However, the insurance company's requirements created an eight-week postponement of my surgery. Eight weeks, two more agonizing months to wait. Two more months for whatever was inside me to fester and grow. Tick-tick-tick.

I was near the end of my ability to cope.

When things seem the bleakest, when despair is encroaching, when all hope seems lost, God has not abandoned us. He demonstrates this Truth in Joshua 1:5 when He promises, *"I will never leave you nor forsake you."* Never means never! Oh, how I needed to focus on that. And, oh, how I needed the love and strength Bill enveloped me in. And, oh, how I needed the prayer and support of my family and friends. And, oh, how they gave it.

As soon as the postponement of my surgery became known, the rally began. I was in pretty desperate shape so those around me literally "lifted me." There is simply no way to describe how this ministered to me. I felt like I was in the very lap of my heavenly Father. I felt His mighty arms about me through the physical touch of my precious husband, family and friends. Hidden *"in the shadow of Thy wings…"* (Psalm 17:8^NASB)

The parents of the students in Sarah's class were extremely close. We were all very involved and very supportive of the school. Many of the students in Sarah's class had siblings in Amy's class also, and that just increased our interaction with one another. Our Christian school was fairly small, but quite active and all of our lives were truly connected. And also truly busy.

But not too busy to support me. Cheryl, the mother of a girl in Sarah's class and a boy in Amy's, plus a preschooler and a small baby (now that's a busy woman!) organized and hosted a prayer time in her home to pray specifically for me.

I clearly remember Cheryl's petitions and the tender words of the other mothers. I was deeply moved by their prayers. I remember the warmth of their hands on my arms and shoulders as they touched me, encircling me, and prayed over me…I remember them saying things like "Chris, you are fearfully and wonderfully made…He knows exactly what's happening within your body even now…He knows every hair on your head, Chris…He knows your name… He cares for you…He is with you…He fills you…He loves you…" I remember them quoting Scripture over me. They spoke blessings over me. They asked for complete healing.

And, when I needed them most, there were countless encouraging phone calls and notes. Support was demonstrated in numerous creative ways. Barbara made "prayer bears" by painting clothes pins and attaching a tiny furry bear to each one. My friends clipped them to their clothes as a reminder to pray for me. Beth and her children drew cheerful decorations on a pillowcase for me to use in the hospital. Susan gave me a little stuffed bunny with mini-bandages crisscrossed over its chest to be my mastectomy partner.

And then there was "The Brunch." I can't remember exactly who originated the idea, but the mothers of the students in Sarah and Amy's classes got all decked out and met at a lovely local restaurant for a special brunch in my honor. Well, that's not completely accurate. Actually…

Nearly thirty of us gathered at the restaurant. Once we were seated, we offered prayer and then click, click, click our heels resounded on the marble floor as we made our way through the sumptuous buffet. Once we returned and were settled at our table, the wait staff checked on us. Yes, thank you, juice would be wonderful.

Cold, freshly-squeezed orange juice appeared in beautiful goblets. Someone raised a glass and said, "I'd like to propose a toast." What a great idea…up go all of our glasses and the toast was offered, "So long lefty, so long righty!"

Nearly thirty finely dressed ladies immediately burst into raucous laughter! We knew precisely what that meant, but the waiter was a bit confused. Wanting to be part of the obvious fun we were enjoying, he asked someone what we were celebrating. I know he was expecting to hear that a birthday or anniversary or similar milestone was the event that brought us all together with such glee. He was a bit bemused by our responses.

We delicately described that I was about to undergo a surgical procedure and we celebrate because we know God is in control. We celebrate because God has a great sense of humor. We celebrate because we love one another. We celebrate because God is faithful. When we focus on Truth and on Jesus, our hearts naturally overflow with joy.

We certainly made an impression on him, and he took wonderful care of us that morning. And my dear friends took wonderful care of me. The brunch, which became forevermore affectionately known as "The Boob Brunch," was a farewell salute to my breasts…alas, we bade a fond farewell to "lefty" and "righty" and I, bathed in love, support and prayer, prepared to send them off in style!

And the eight long weeks passed.

CHAPTER ELEVEN

A House in Order

I had had plenty of time to think about the reality of what I might be facing. I believe it's a normal reaction to expect the best, but prepare for the worst-case scenario. I had prepared for the possibility that I could die.

In the event of my death, I wanted to donate any of my organs or body parts which could possibly be of use, even if just for medical research. I planned my memorial service. I chose songs. I wrote a letter to be read aloud to my family and friends. And I wrote personal letters to each of my two beloved daughters. I shared my dreams for them in their individual letters. I described as best I could the joy they brought into my life. I presented my favorite Scripture verses and the ones I saw come to life through both of them. I gave them "motherly advice" and basically said all I felt I needed to say. I emptied the words that flooded my heart. And I told them that because of the assurance of salvation, I knew I would be with them again one day.

Then I wrote a farewell love letter to Bill. It was the most difficult letter I have ever written in my life. Its contents are far too personal to share.

Lastly, I had a "meeting" with Bill to discuss my final arrangements. I wanted to cover all the details, including my favorite flowers. The meeting had lasted about two seconds when Bill interrupted it. "Chris, I just can't talk about this." He pleaded. But I insisted. He indulged me because he didn't want to upset me and because he knew I really needed to get it all out. So he mercifully listened to me go on and on presenting my wishes.

Then, in what I considered to be my most valiant sacrifice, I made him promise me that he would marry again. Sarah and Amy, after all, needed a loving mother, and he needed a companion to share his life. I didn't want him to be alone. I meant this from the bottom of my heart.

Bill was really squirming around in his seat by now. "Chris, I don't want to think about this. YOU are my wife." "Please, I need you to promise me you will remarry." He tried his best to continue our unbearable conversation. I continued to say all I needed to say. In the event of his remarriage, I had only one absolute stipulation. His future bride must have no children of her own, but be a devoted, godly mother to Sarah and Amy. Oh, and there was just one other minor stipulation as well. She had to sleep in a separate bedroom from Bill and he had to promise to keep MY photo next to him on his night stand forever!

I didn't think that was asking too much! ☺

CHAPTER TWELVE

When We
Least Expect It

Other preparations were necessary as well.

My doctor and I had discussed some of the details and possible complications of the upcoming surgery. Consequently, he encouraged me to undergo a procedure to extract and reserve adequate quantities of my own blood. In the event of hemorrhage or other condition requiring a blood transfusion, my own blood would be available to administer. Obviously, this would eliminate any concern over incompatibility or risk of contracting an undetected disease from an anonymous blood source.

Arrangements were made and I arrived at the Red Cross center to "donate" blood to myself. I completed the forms and made my way from station-to-station in the clinical process. Eventually, I met with a counselor to review my paperwork. She carefully studied the details of my case, performed her duties and discussed the next steps with me. I confirmed my awareness of exactly what was happening both that day and in the near future.

In the midst of our discussion, she placed my paperwork back down on her desk, removed her glasses and looked me right in the eyes. "Mrs. Weaver, you are very calm as you discuss this," she said. I think she wanted to be certain that I actually understood the gravity of the situation I faced. I don't recall exactly what I said, but I know I expressed to her that I most definitely understood and that I was at total peace because I knew Jesus was in control of the entire situation as well as its ultimate outcome. I know I told her that I was thankful to be able to have the mastectomies because I viewed the procedure as a solution to my problem and not THE problem.

Her next statement made a lasting impression on me.

She said that by the time she meets with them, most women in my situation are in a state of great anxiety and trepidation combined with deep depression. She said there is undisputed scientific evidence that women with a mind-set of hopefulness recover more quickly and have a more positive post-surgical outcome than those who don't. She said she expected I'd do well since I seemed to have such a "good attitude." I couldn't help but think of the mind-body connection 1 Thessalonians 5:23 presents and how man's scientific studies confirm God's Truth. Praise God for the relevance and practical application of Scripture! *"Now may the God of peace Himself sanctify you entirely; and may your spirit and soul and body be preserved complete, without blame at the coming of our Lord Jesus Christ."* (1 Thessalonians 5:23[NASB])

With joy in my heart and a smile on my face, I repeated my profession of faith in Jesus Christ as the source of my strength and peace that passes understanding.

She wished me well and signed off on my paperwork and cleared me to proceed to the next step of the blood donation process.

As I sat at the final station, the juice and cookie station, I chatted with some of the other donors who had overheard my previous conversation.

When we least expect it, Jesus can even use our most troublesome circumstances to encourage and minister Truth to us, and through us, to those whose paths we cross. What a privilege and tender blessing. To God be the glory!

CHAPTER THIRTEEN

Maybe I'm Not as Ready as I Thought I Was

At long last, we sat in church on the final Sunday morning before my surgery. My pre-op visit was scheduled for the following morning and then surgery on Tuesday.

As part of the Sunday morning worship, our church closed the service with the same uplifting song each week. We sang it and clapped along as we filed out of the sanctuary.

> *"My life is in You, Lord.*
> *My strength is in You, Lord.*
> *My hope is in You, Lord.*
> *In You, It's in You.*
> *In You, It's in You. It's in You!"*

I had sung that chorus a million times; but I heard the words for the first time that Sunday morning. The lyrics were my reality. Face-to-face with reality, I wept hard as I sang. My very life WAS in His hands and I knew it. My only hope was in Him. Emotion welled within me.

Typically, the pre-op visit is nothing remarkable. Fill out a few forms, have some blood drawn and undergo an electrocardiogram. Pretty standard stuff. I had been down that road many times before. I knew what to expect.

Or so I thought. I didn't expect that I would feel so much fear this time. The members of our Sunday school class had prayed for me on Sunday and their prayer support was actually palpable. I was feeling so secure that I hadn't even accepted Bill's offer to go to the hospital with me that morning.

I had been fine when I left home, so perhaps that's why I was so unsettled by my increasing fear as the process commenced. I remember how oddly matter-of-fact everyone was. "Here are your pre-op instructions. Be sure to read them and remember the doctor wants you to take this sleeping pill tonight." Then off I went to the next department. "Mrs. Weaver, please read this release form and sign it at the bottom." I signed the form giving the hospital permission to remove my left and right breasts, and which released everyone from responsibility in the event of my death. Next stop: the Lab. Then on to Radiology. I remember the eerie sound of my steps as I walked the vast and cavernous hall from place to place. I was alone in the corridors, and my footsteps resounded as if I were one of the Rockettes at Radio City Music Hall.

Unfortunately, I was not a world-renown dancer in the midst of a show-stopping performance. I was just a woman facing the reality of losing part of herself and embracing the unknown.

By the time I walked out of the revolving hospital doors, I was engrossed in my own little world of worry and was most startled as I heard a familiar voice cheerfully calling my name. "Hi there, Chris!" I looked up and standing in front of me was another angel sent to minister to me in my time of need.

With a huge smile on his face, our Associate Pastor, Mike, had come to the hospital to visit a church member who had just had a baby. He "just happened" to cross my path at that precise moment! We chatted briefly and then parted to resume our separate activities. His easy smile and the cheerful lilt in his voice stayed with me.

The encounter was further evidence of how intimately Jesus knows me. He affirmed His abiding presence with me and quieted my soul. He promised that He will never leave me or forsake me and I knew I was not at the hospital "alone" after all. He even sent me someone with "skin on" to prove it! God is our refuge and our strength, a very present help in times of trouble. My fear was replaced with rejoicing. I drove home singing praises to His name.

LouAnn, whose two daughters were classmates of Sarah and Amy, had picked the girls up after school and had invited them to spend the night at her home. Bill and I could get a good night's sleep and we knew LouAnn would tenderly care for our girls and drive them to school with her own girls the next morning. Laurie, another class mother, would pick them up from school and bring them to her home so Bill could remain with me at the hospital after the surgery. Laurie had even stopped by when I returned from the pre-op visit to deliver a poster-sized card signed by our entire Sunday school class and also by the parents of the girls' school classes. Our church sponsored the Christian School Sarah and Amy attended and it was housed in the same building. It was very much a family.

I took the sleeping pill and actually slept that night.

Chapter Fourteen

This is the Day

My memory of the day of surgery is fragmented at best. I remember that Bill and I had been taken back to the pre-op area. I recall lying on the gurney already garbed in the fashionable backless hospital gown, matching booties and cap. I am certain that I had an IV running in my arm because I was already feeling pretty "happy." I vaguely remember our Pastor standing next to Bill. I remember my doctor coming in and how relieved Bill looked, but then I fade out and Bill's memory takes over for a moment.

It was around 6:30 a.m. when our Pastor arrived at the hospital to pray with us before the surgery. It meant so much to me to have him there. We prayed for Chris and for her doctor and for a positive outcome of the procedure. Chris was getting pretty drowsy and when the doctor arrived, our Pastor excused himself.

The doctor entered the little room and reviewed Chris' chart. He asked if I had any questions and then asked me if it would be all right if he offered a word of prayer. He GOT DOWN ON HIS KNEES and prayed for God's

*wisdom and specifically asked that God would open his
eyes and guide his hands as he performed the surgery on
Chris. What a unique and profound experience to share
with a doctor!*

I remember seeing one after another of the overhead lights
as the nurse rolled my gurney down the hall toward the
operating room. Bill was rapidly walking beside the gurney,
holding my hand, and I remember thinking, "Was this the
last time I would ever see this precious man's face?"

The nurse very sensitively told us that we had reached the
spot where we must part company. Bill leaned down and
we kissed and professed our love for one another. And the
nurse wheeled me off to the left and Bill walked straight
ahead to the waiting area.

I remember being concerned that Bill would be alone
during my surgical procedure. Once again, the Lord
eliminated that concern immediately.

The huge steel door the nurse had just wheeled me through
swung back open just enough for me to catch a glimpse of
Penny's husband, Jim, scooting down the hall toward the
surgical waiting area. Jim and Penny had been our Sunday
school teachers when we were still single, and through the
many years since then we have remained close friends.
I knew Bill was blessed in Jim's wonderful company and
I was at peace and in awe of my all-knowing God.

I was in a little holding area, waiting to go into the operating
room. I saw figures dressed in hospital blues scurrying

around. One figure came over to my gurney and pulled back her surgical mask just enough to reveal her identity. It was my doctor's nurse. "Hello, Christine. How are you doing? We're ready for you. The doctor will be here in a moment and then we'll wheel you into the operating room." She introduced me to a few other members of the team, and I think I remember the anesthetist greeting me. I think I remember seeing my doctor. I definitely recall that everyone seemed calm and totally focused on me. It was very reassuring and comforting.

Again, my memory fades and Bill recalls his.

> *I kissed Chris and told her I loved her. The nurse instructed me to proceed to the waiting area and informed me that someone would be keeping me appraised of the situation. In a bit of a daze, I walked over to the surgical waiting area. It was a difficult moment to see Chris wheeled away. I couldn't help but wonder if I'd ever see her again. What would life be like from this point on? God, I surrender her into Your hands. There is nothing more I can do.*

> *I arrived at the waiting area and I was about to sit down when I looked up and saw our friend Jim coming down the hall toward me. Praise God, what a welcome sight! Jim quickly said, "Let's go get some breakfast." So we went to the hospital's cafeteria. We prayed, but Jim was careful to keep the conversation light. Jim talked and kept my mind occupied, although I must admit that my head was spinning. After eating, we returned to the waiting area.*

Jim did not leave my side. So much emphasis and attention had been focused on Chris' health situation, with good reason, and it was very natural for me to be strong for Chris. I hadn't realized until this moment how deeply I also needed support. Jim's presence was a true blessing to me.

I heard someone calling out, "Christine…Christine… Christine…" and I remember saying in an almost annoyed tone of voice, "What do you WANT?" I opened my eyes and there stood my doctor and another man, still wearing their surgical scrubs. They had a slight look of shock on their faces after my response! My doctor very calmly said, "I want you to slide over onto this gurney."

I came to my senses a bit. I was embarrassed at how sternly I had responded to his call. I guess I was dreaming… anyway, with their assistance, I did my best to maneuver myself over onto the gurney with tubes and monitors and drains attached to me.

My doctor said that both he and the anesthesiologist were surprised that I had awakened from surgery so quickly. He told me the surgery was over and I was now going to be taken to the recovery area. He was going to the waiting area to speak with Bill. His voice was reassuring and calm and comforting. I drifted back to sleep.

Several hours passed and the doctor finally emerged from the surgical area. He walked over to where Jim and I were sitting and let us know that Chris came through

*the surgery well and was now in the recovery area. He
indicated that he had removed SEVERAL breast tumors,
which indeed were present. It was a bit of a surprise to
learn that the doctor also removed all but one of Chris'
lymph nodes as well. He said he "didn't like the way
they looked." So now I was not only concerned about
the findings on Chris' tumors, the lymph involvement
presented further complications. The doctor assured me
that while it will take some time for the in-depth pathology
reports, the preliminary findings appeared to be good.
He was kind and cheerful and let me know he'd speak
with me again in a few hours.*

*Soon a nurse informed us that Chris had been assigned a
room and would be transported to it shortly. She said we
were welcome to go on ahead and wait for Chris there.
Jim and I proceeded to Chris' hospital room to await her
arrival.*

I have no memory of being in the recovery area. No
memory of nurses or doctors or any sounds or activity.
I vaguely remember being wheeled into my private hospital
room and have a slight recollection of Bill and Jim already
sitting there.

I do, however, have quite a vivid memory of a lovely, fresh
floral arrangement displayed on the table facing my hospital
bed. I asked about it and the nurse said the flowers were
from my doctor and his staff! "He always wants flowers to
be waiting in the room when his patients are brought up
from recovery."

It seems almost unbelievable, doesn't it? But it is true. I wonder if my doctor and his staff will ever know the full impact of their kindness and sensitivity. I know Jesus does.

Chris arrived in her hospital room and Jim spoke to her briefly, but Chris was still very groggy. He left soon after she arrived. I was so grateful for his company. God bless that man.

The nurses helped Chris become situated in the hospital bed and adjusted various tubes and IV lines and drains and devices so she would be as comfortable as possible. Chris drifted in and out of consciousness. I called her parents and my mother to update them on her condition and inform them of the latest information I had.

I remember sleeping on my back, occasionally waking to see Bill faithfully sitting in a chair, watching me from the corner of the room. His presence was assuring and comforting. I think I kept opening my eyes just to be sure he was still there. He was.

I also have a distinct memory of Kitty's face. Leaning over me, she softly said, "Chris, look at my eyes. I had to come see you." She brought me a wooden angel ornament and hung it on my IV pole. Little did she know what an angel SHE was in my life!

Kitty said something to Bill, but I drifted in and out of consciousness and don't really remember anything else of that day or night.

I sat there watching Chris as she drifted in and out of consciousness. I was exhausted, but was afraid to fall asleep. What if something happened to Chris? What if no one wakes me up? What if someone comes to visit Chris? I needed to be alert so I could answer their questions and report what little I knew at this time. I forced myself to stay in control.

Even though I was worn out, my body wouldn't let me drift off to sleep. I found myself thinking about what lies ahead. So much of my energy and effort had been focused on getting to this point that I hadn't allowed myself to think beyond the surgery. I'd been dealing with all the insurance issues, preparing for the girls to be cared for and handling many other details. Not to mention my job demands. Certainly, my priority was Chris, but it was my business and I couldn't just completely leave my clients and work unattended. Now that the surgery was over, the reality of what could lie ahead started to rise to the surface.

The pathologist who was present in the operating room did preliminary testing, but the final analysis was still days away.

As much as I didn't want to think about it, I kept wondering if Chris actually had cancer. Did they remove it all? Would Chris be okay or will our lives be different from this point on? Will life ever be normal again?

It wasn't long before Chris' nurse came into her room. She presented her first-hand report of the surgery. She was so kind, and knowing of their faith in God brought even more comfort and reassurance. Not surprisingly, she described the doctor's thorough and careful operating procedure. She was right at his side and reported that when he examined the tissue looking for the tumor Chris had been feeling, the surgical team actually gasped when he located it because of its large size. When he examined Chris' other breast, it was so dense with tumors he stopped counting them and just removed the tissue so the pathologist could perform the frozen sections.

She confirmed the doctor's initial findings that all looked good at this point, but we wouldn't know for sure until the complete pathology report was issued.

She briefly checked on Chris, but she was not awake so the nurse said she'd stop by again that evening.

CHAPTER FIFTEEN

La-La Land

The effects of the anesthesia began to diminish and, although groggy, I slowly regained consciousness. I recall pulling open my hospital gown to check my upper torso. I saw drains and a surgical dressing covering what appeared to be an otherwise rather normal-looking body.

I was still receiving intravenous fluid and medication. An additional tube was attached to my arm, and my hand clutched a device I vaguely recalled my nurse mentioning. Surprisingly, I had some discomfort, but really no pain.

Bill explained that the device was attached to a morphine pump which enabled me to self-administer the pain medication. Simply push the little button and a pre-measured dose of the drug would be immediately dispensed. Wow.

Apparently a patient recovering in the room adjacent to mine was also attached to a morphine pump. I could hear the faint "ping" sound of her machine responding and activating as she pushed the device she clutched in her hand. Although I was not in pain, each time I heard her morphine pump kick in I pushed my little button as well! Whoosh, the morphine was on its merry way to my bloodstream and I would again drift off into la-la land. As the medicine subsided, I would eventually resume awareness. Ping! My neighbor's pump would ring again and in a Pavlovian response, I'd push my little button as well. Whoosh, came my morphine dose and back to la-la land I'd go. This little pattern continued until during one moment of resumed lucidity, I realized I was actually not in any pain whatsoever and, therefore, did not need the morphine. So I stopped pushing my little red button no matter how many times her little "ping" resounded.

The nurses tending to me reviewed the machine's data output and eventually disconnected and removed my morphine pump. I wasn't even using it, but I remember thinking, "Oh, no! Don't take that away!"

It's a bit disconcerting to realize how easy it would be to surrender control of one's mind and body to a drug. I certainly appreciate my doctor and the nurses who watched over me and removed my morphine pump at the appropriate time.

CHAPTER SIXTEEN

Up, Up and Away

My doctor was extremely positive and pleased with the outcome of the surgery and my immediate post-surgical topical healing. The nurses were similarly upbeat. The care I received was compassionate and professional. To a person, the hospital staff was consistently pleasant and kind. I was deeply touched by the tender care, but I was, after all, recuperating in the hospital not enjoying a trip to the spa.

Reality was reality. Although preliminary reports were good, much was still unknown and inconclusive.

The tissue and tumors and lymph nodes which were removed from my body were still being analyzed and tested by the pathologists. The written report would not be available for two more days...two more grueling days of anticipation. More waiting.

We all did our best to continue to trust God with all of our hearts and keep our focus on Truth and avoid the "elephant in the room." Honestly, I think I was so relieved to finally have the tumors out of my body, I already felt a huge sense of relief. The ticking "time-bombs" were voided and could no longer explode and destroy me. Of course, I prayed that there would be no residual effects of their presence. Prayed and waited.

Waiting, however, did not translate to resting! My doctor wanted me up and out of that hospital bed. Sitting. Walking. Moving. I really did not feel like sitting or walking or moving. I was not in pain, but I was sore and uncomfortable. I still had drains and an IV line attached. It took constant prompting from the nurses to motivate me...I really just wanted to remain in "royal" repose. Ha!

With my nurse's assistance, I s-l-o-w-l-y managed to maneuver myself completely out of the bed. As I stood in a semi-upright position for the first time, I could immediately detect the shift in my balance due to the removal of my breasts. I had a difficult time finding my center of gravity. It was an odd and unfamiliar sensation.

Leaning first on my bed and then the bedside chair, my first tentative steps marked a significant milestone in my recovery process. Still weak, I felt like a baby bird leaving the security of its nest.

I carefully inched my way around the hospital room, pushing my IV pole, as I scooted over to the window. Reflected in the glass was my first full view of my altered, post-surgical, reconstructed body. The difference was obvious to me but I never, not even for a second, "felt like a freak." Those were my exact words. I became acutely aware that the silicone implants enabled me to look like a woman and not a "freak."

It's a significant and particularly devastating loss, the loss of breasts.

CHAPTER SEVENTEEN

Reality and Remembrance

The blur of the first post-operative days evolved into a steady course of recovery and I was awake more than I was asleep. Still sore and fragile, I gradually grew in stamina.

My parents and Bill's mother, who generously took turns caring for Sarah and Amy so Bill could visit me, came to the hospital when the girls were in school.

Each morning and each evening my doctor visited my hospital room to examine me, check my progress, keep me updated and informed and address any concerns or questions I might have.

I did have many questions. Was my body rejecting the implants? Were there any signs of infection? How long did the drains need to remain? Lots of questions… about anything and everything…with the exception of those pertaining to the "elephant in the room."

But it could no longer be ignored or avoided. The pathology report had been completed.

I reached for Bill's hand as we intently listened to my doctor present the findings. He utilized somewhat technical medical terminology, but we understood that the laboratory analysis confirmed his initial report. My heart pounding, I heard only disjointed words like "hot spots" and "looked bad" and "unremarkable" and "on time," but Bill heard the bottom line:

Tests on the tumors, tissue and lymph nodes revealed the presence of pre-cancerous cells, but no chemotherapy was recommended at this time. No radiation. No need to meet with an oncologist. No further surgery at this time. We could breathe again.

Alone in my hospital bed that evening, I began to process the reality of my doctor's report and remembered the milestones leading up to it.

I remembered being completely unaware of the tumor until Spice stepped directly onto it; that "hidden" tumor no one else ever felt or mammograms revealed. I remembered all the doctor visits and examinations and inconclusive test results. I remembered the woman from the magazine. I remembered Kitty's endless "call a doctor" phone calls. I remembered the unusual and rather peculiar set of circumstances ultimately directing me to my current doctor. I remembered Bill's tearful description of his kneeling before my gurney, asking the Great Physician to guide his hands and eyes and mind as he performed my surgical procedure. I remembered all the prayer petitions lifted before the Throne of Grace on my behalf. And I remembered the words, "PRE-cancerous" and "on time."

Before I had any knowledge of danger, my Savior knew. When I didn't know where to turn, my Lord guided me. When circumstances seemed hopeless, my Jesus restored me. When I was fearful, my Comforter quieted my soul.

"Great is Thy faithfulness, oh God, my Father.
Morning by morning, new mercies I see…
ALL I have needed, Thy hand hath provided…
Great is Thy faithfulness, Lord, unto me."

Chapter Eighteen

May I Have Your Autograph?

Word of the pathology results spread like wildfire and the praises resounded! Thank You, Jesus!

Phone calls, cards, flowers, gifts and well wishes literally flooded my hospital room. And then the parade began.

The parade of visitors, that is. My parents, Bill's mother, extended family members, fellow church members, neighbors, friends, the wife of my former doctor, my current doctor's nursing staff (who came before and after working at his office…visiting me on their PERSONAL time).

Then the mothers arrived. One-by-one, and sometimes two-by-two, my "Boob Brunch" buddies, the mothers of Sarah and Amy's classmates, came to spend a few moments with me while their children were in school. I cherished their visits.

Unbeknownst to me, for security purposes, all visitors were

required to register at the hospital's information/reception desk located in the lobby prior to being permitted on patient floors.

Soon I began to notice a few "new" faces glancing into my room followed by the sound of their whispers outside my door. Then one day an unknown woman entered my room and sat herself right down in my visitor's chair. Sensing my apprehension, she identified herself as the hospital receptionist and said so many visitors had checked in with her, so many cards and flowers delivered to my room, that the hospital staff was actually talking about it, wondering who their "CELEBRITY" patient was. She decided to come check it out for herself! We laughed over that!

Actually, we laughed quite a bit during her initial visit and she began to visit me more often...eventually utilizing her breaks and lunchtimes to briefly stop by my room. Although we covered a variety of subjects during our casual chats, an amazing opportunity arose from her initial curiosity as to my identity. I was able to share about who all the visitors were. I told her about their prayer support and attempted to describe "the fellowship of the saints." I shared my faith, the reason for my peace, which had made a distinct impression on her.

To be completely honest, I wouldn't have described myself as someone who sought after evangelistic opportunities. Not in a million years. I am truly a shy person and most definitely preferred being behind the scenes. My theory was, "I'll offer the prayer support as *you* share your faith." Who was this new person I had become? Suddenly I was "testifying" at the drop of a hat! Hmm, perhaps sharing my faith wasn't so terrifying after all...actually, it's a rather natural response to God's faithfulness. He even brings people right to your bedside to hear His message of hope! Pretty cool.

My family and friends simply set out to visit me, but their efforts were not only tender blessings to me, virtual strangers were impacted by the enormity of God's unconditional love demonstrated via their sacrifices. And I was privileged to "witness" about it.

It's just awesome to realize that the "puzzle pieces" of our individual lives fit together perfectly into the Master's plan!

What a mighty God we serve...

CHAPTER NINETEEN

Mmmmm!

I was sore and tender, weak and fragile; my body still recovering from the trauma of the surgery and subsequent reconstruction. The dressing over my wounds was still present, but much easier to manage. The drains were still attached. I was progressively recuperating, but finally, I was HOME!

For eight weeks I would not be permitted to drive, lift anything heavier than five pounds, sleep on my stomach, or go without wearing the special supportive undergarments I'd worn continuously since my surgery. For a wife and mother of two young daughters, some of these instructions presented a real challenge. Once again, these obstacles were immediately overcome with sights, sounds, smells and tastes that will last in my heart forever.

My father and Bill's mother shared the responsibility of carpooling Sarah and Amy to and from school. Bill helped the girls with their homework and school projects. My mother helped me bathe, did our laundry, helped prepare the girls' lunches and "baby-sat" me once Bill returned to work. Jackie washed my kitchen floor on her hands and knees. Laurie recorded a customized cassette tape of instrumental favorites and titled it, "Music To Heal By." Cindy took the girls to ballet class. Notes and cards continued to arrive. And Beth arranged for meals for our family. She made a sign-up chart and, again, the classroom mothers, teachers, staff and church members rallied to help us. For eight weeks, TWO MONTHS, delicious home-cooked meals were delivered to our family. Sometimes little gifts for the girls were tucked into the food baskets, wrapped in pretty napkins.

There was a popular "fact" circulating at that time that American families ate most of their meals at fast-food restaurants rather than at home. Sadly, that hadn't been terribly far from the truth at our home.

I used to jokingly say that when I called the girls for dinner, they'd pick up their little purses and head for the garage instead of the dinner table. They thought food came from the car, not from the kitchen! I've never claimed to be a great cook, but things weren't quite that extreme. However, I did learn a pretty graphic lesson once the home-cooked meals started arriving.

Our master bedroom was on the upper level of our home. Bill set up a little bed for me on the couch in our den so I would only have to negotiate the stairs once a day. One evening I was resting in the den when our dinner arrived. The aroma of the meal was indescribable. Beef roast with onion gravy, cheesy potato casserole, pistachio congealed salad, fresh-baked buttered rolls, and a homemade chocolate pie, still warm, right out of the oven. I'm not kidding. Bill and the girls practically ran to the table and all I heard coming from the dining room was absolute silence, broken only by the occasional, enthusiastic, "Mmmmmm!"

I would love to report that this only happened one time. Nope. In came a homemade chicken potpie baked in a homemade crust. Cheese-filled lasagna. Homemade Chinese food complete with pot stickers. Casseroles. Pork Roasts. Salads. Homemade breads and muffins and brownies and cookies and cakes galore.

As thankful as I was (more thankful than my words could ever convey) for the nutritious meals being provided for my family, I was definitely feeling the pressure!

Was this normal? Do people really eat like this on a Tuesday night? Had my friends secretly been abducted and "Stepford Wives" were masquerading in their place? Just when I was feeling like the world's worst wife, one of the delivery men (a husband) spilled the beans!

As Bill and the girls reenacted their nightly ritual of perusing the incoming feast, verbalizing their delight with drool spilling down their chins, my friend's husband said, "I know, this does smell delicious. This is one of my wife's specialties and one of our family's favorite dinners. She made this for you tonight, but we're having hot dogs!" Hallelujah! I felt better already.

These women were making their very BEST meals for us! I entered into the daily celebration with Bill, Sarah and Amy as I pictured my dear friends shopping, preparing and delivering the spectacular meals to us so we would be cared for and pleased. They were cooking as unto the Lord. Tears filled my eyes with each delivery. Bless them, Father.

(NOTE: I am writing this book nearly twenty years after these events occurred. Tonight I asked my husband to proofread this chapter and when he was finished, his only comment was, "I remember that meal!"

My friend graciously allowed me to share her recipe for the roast. I've served it many, many times over the years and I think of her kindness each and every time I do. I pray it blesses you and your family as well. Enjoy!)

Carole's Quick Chuck Roast

4 lb. chuck roast
1 oz. bottle steak sauce
1 package dry onion soup mix
1 can 98% fat-free cream of mushroom soup

Remove all visible fat and place roast onto a LARGE sheet of aluminum foil. Pierce roast all over with a fork. Pour the entire bottle of steak sauce over the roast being careful to keep the sauce on the meat/foil. Pour dry onion soup mix over meat and using a spatula combine soup mix with steak sauce to form a "paste" on the roast. Next "frost" the roast with the cream of mushroom soup. (Note: This will not LOOK particularly appetizing at this stage, but trust me, it will taste great!)

Wrap the roast completely in the aluminum foil. Use several additional sheets if necessary. (This keeps the gravy from escaping.) Place the foil-wrapped meat in a roasting pan and cook at 350 degrees for three hours. Remove from the oven and, still wrapped, allow the meat to "rest" for thirty minutes before serving.

CHAPTER TWENTY

Nurse Nancy

When I was a little girl I loved to read. One of my favorite books was entitled, "Nurse Nancy." The book was about a little girl named Nancy. Dressed in a cute little blue-and-white striped nurse's outfit, complete with hat and blue cape, "Nurse Nancy" took care of her cat as well as various other animals. It made me want to become a nurse when I grew up. (I never did.)

Before I went into the hospital to undergo my surgery, I made little nurse caps for Sarah and Amy and stashed them away. I thought it would be fun for them to wear those hats and "take care" of me upon my return home. I knew I wouldn't feel up to playing with them and I hoped this would provide an opportunity for the girls to "play" nurse and patient with me.

That actually happened and it was a sweet time. Sarah and Amy wore their little nurse caps, put paper towels over cookie sheets and used them as trays to bring me juice and special little treats they had prepared. They used straws and pretended to take my temperature. They drew me pictures and sat with me and read me stories. They actually took very good care of me. Just like Nurse Nancy.

To make a simple little nurse cap, follow these easy instructions:

- You will need one 12 x 18 inch sheet of white paper.

- Hold the paper vertically and fold it in half, with the crease at the top.

- Now fold both upper corners down until they meet at the center.

- Fold the flaps remaining at the bottom up on each side to secure the hat form.

- Use a non-toxic marker to draw a red cross on the front of the brim.

- Gently open the cap and your little nurse will be ready to see her first patient!

CHAPTER TWENTY-ONE

Potpourri

Although I was home, I was still on medication and became a bit "loopy" and "drifty" from it at times. During the day I was often so drowsy I fell fast asleep on the little bed in the den that Bill made me.

One day I was apparently out cold on my little den-bed when our doorbell rang. One of the "Nurse Nancys" ran full speed and opened the door before I could stop her. In walked our mailman. There I was in all my glory, sprawled out, eyes spinning wildly, still babbling incoherently as he handed me a letter requiring a receipt signature. I'm sure he had some interesting thoughts as he got back into his truck.

On another occasion, my friend Jill came to visit me. Still worried about the possible rejection or hardening of my implants, I forced her to feel my breasts to be sure they weren't getting rigid. Somewhere in the back of my altered mind I thought she had once been a nurse. I figured any nurse, past or present, would be able to perform the infamous breast-hardness test. I think poor Jill mumbled something about working as an attendant at a nursing home when she was in high school, but she had never been a nurse. I didn't give Jill a break. I guess I thought that was close enough to being a nurse and proceeded to unbutton my robe. She just gave in, indulged me and told me my breasts felt just fine to her. I'm sure Jill had some choice thoughts when she got into her car as well.

Another friend, along with her mother who had also recently undergone mastectomies, stopped in to visit me one afternoon. I had never met my friend's mother before.

Within seconds of our meeting, before they had even put their purses down and to my friend's absolute shock and horror, her mother and I were both exposing our new bodies to one another. I'm sure they also had an interesting conversation on their way home.

On another morning, I received a phone call from Amy's first-grade teacher. I distinctly remember our conversation. Who could ever forget a conversation like this one:

"Mrs. Weaver, is there something going on at your home that I should know about?"

"Nothing other than what you're already aware of. Why?"

"Well, I got a phone call from Sam's mother last night. Apparently Sam came home from school and told his mother that Amy's mother had her breasts cut off and

Mr. Weaver had them mounted and hung them on their bedroom wall."

"What??????"

"I think that was her reaction as well. So she put in a call to me. I thought I should check with you personally."

I assured Amy's teacher that my husband had no such trophies on display in our bedroom or anywhere else for that matter.

Somewhere I had read that children are the best recorders of information, but the worst interpreters of information. I should say so! Poor Amy. No telling what she was reporting at school.

My actions were rather strange to say the least! I can only attribute this to a sudden hormonal imbalance or the reaction to the stress of surgery or the prescription medications I was taking...or something...because my behavior definitely took a bizarre tack for a time.

Without getting too graphic, due to the discharge and other symptoms and complications I had suffered prior to my surgery, it was necessary to remove all of my breast tissue, skin and "accessories" during the operation. My doctor had stitched little pockets under my arms to grow my own tissue to be harvested in a subsequent surgery. This would then be formed into reconstructed areola and nipples, tattooed to look completely authentic, and then "installed."

My doctor clinically referred to these tissue pockets as "flesh farms." Meanwhile, I still had a "blank slate" shall we say. I told Bill this was as close as I'd ever come to looking just like Barbie!

One day, in my medication stupor, I borrowed two tiny pink pompons, called foosballs, from the girls' toy bin and scotch taped them to my body in the appropriate spots. Use your imagination. When Bill walked into the room I flung open my shirt and shouted, "Surprise!" I can still remember the astonished look on his face and the enormous gasp he uttered. I'm sure he had a few unpleasant words in his mind when he left the room as well.

I needed the medication so discontinuing its use was not an option. Instead, Bill gently reminded me that I needed to get myself together. He said, "Chris, look down at your chest. These are not toys, these are BREASTS. You need to stop unbuttoning your shirt every time someone walks into the room!" He wasn't kidding.

Bill helped me to realize that I actually had no emotional connection to these reconstructed mounds located on my chest. My breasts were gone. And, due to the surgery, I couldn't even feel my chest any longer. The nerve endings had been severed. So, subconsciously, I categorized the implants as I would any other fashion accessory…rather like a nice pair of new shoes.

This was another heartbreaking revelation for me. My breasts were gone forever. I grieved their loss. The factory-made artificial counterparts were their permanent replacements and I needed to force myself to emotionally receive them.

One night I woke up with a sharp pain shooting through my chest. It literally took my breath away. In the morning, it happened again. It felt just like the pain I experienced when Spice stepped on me that Saturday morning. When I called my doctor to report this unsettling pain, he told me what I was experiencing was normal. It was "phantom pain." It's a common occurrence experienced at one time or another by all amputees. AMPUTEES!!! Is that what I am? An amputee? With everything in me I fought the negative feelings, self-doubt and lies the enemy was whispering to me. I asked the Holy Spirit to comfort me and help me as only He could. I longed to feel feminine and complete again.

I also longed to feel like myself again. And eventually I did. The healing process enabled my body to more easily tolerate the medication, and that helped to stabilize my emotions. Thank goodness! (Can you hear Bill shouting, "Amen" to that?) I learned to just relax and adapt.

Soon I felt well enough and was strong enough to venture out on an actual date with Bill. What a blessing to fix my hair and put on make-up and wear clothing rather than robes. I wore a soft, powder blue skirt and matching top. My blouse had pronounced shoulder pads, which was very much the style in the eighties.

Bill and I went to a lovely quiet restaurant to share a candle-lit meal as a "normal" couple again. It was a wonderful evening.

As we sipped our delicious coffee at the end of the meal, I happened to glance down at my chest and noticed that I had THREE BREASTS! Yes, three. One of my shoulder pads had taken a little vacation, wondered away from my shoulder and settled right smack between my implants…three little maids in a row! I was horrified! No wonder the waiter filled my coffee cup so many times! I asked Bill why he hadn't mentioned this bonus breast to me. He hadn't noticed. Is that not a classic "man moment"? After I discreetly maneuvered the shoulder pad back into place, I made a point of checking things more carefully since I could no longer rely on my sense of feeling…or on my husband's skill of observation!

By the way, since nerve endings are severed it's common to lose feeling after breast surgery. I recently read about a woman who spent hours looking for the remote control to her television set, only to discover she had accidentally rolled over onto it in her sleep and it became lodged between her breast implants. Unbeknownst to her, it was stuck there the entire time she was searching for it!

Sometimes the best medicine is a good laugh!
(Don't worry, in most cases the sense of feeling eventually returns as nerve endings regenerate.)

CHAPTER TWENTY-TWO

No, Please Allow Me

The eight weeks of post-surgical convalescence had come to an end. My doctor was pleased with my progress. My drains were removed, the dressing reduced to small "steri-strips," but I still required the supportive undergarments. I still needed to sleep on my back, holding an additional pillow over my chest.

Actually, I carried that pillow around with me all the time. It provided a little extra support and protection and was a tried-and-true recovery tip my doctor had shared with me. I covered my pillow with the pillowcase Beth's children had decorated for me and named it, "My Buddy."

I was feeling a little better emotionally and definitely more clear-headed and in control.

I had even been given the go-ahead to drive again. My first time driving was yet another memorable experience.

One of the positive consequences of breast surgery is the ripple effect it creates. Other women in your circle of influence are motivated to take their own breast health more seriously. They begin to pay more attention to changes in their bodies. They perform self-examinations.

Incredibly, before the school year was over, three more mothers from our little school would be the guests of honor at their own Boob Brunches. First Barbara, who had distributed the prayer bears at my brunch, would need them herself. Praise God, Barbara's mass was benign.

Next came Jill. Her mother had died of breast cancer when Jill was just sixteen years old. She was so frightened at finding the mass in her own breast she couldn't even bring herself to tell her husband for two weeks. Eventually she did and, Praise God, Jill's growth was benign as well.

But Shelly's was not. Shelly's pathology revealed a late-stage malignancy, and an immediate mastectomy was prescribed.

The impact of Chris' surgery was still fresh on my mind and I was still processing what had happened and what our future held. When I heard about what was going on with Shelly I couldn't help but relate to what her husband, Gregg, was experiencing.

I remembered how comforting it was to have Jim by my side during Chris' surgery. I offered my company to Gregg, but he insisted he'd be fine. But I had thought the same thing. When the day of Shelly's surgery arrived, I knew Gregg would need me so I went to the hospital to be with him. I know Gregg was very glad to see me and

I was happy to be there for him. So much attention is focused on the women, of course, but I was keenly aware that we husbands really need support as well. I know Gregg was thankful that I had decided to come.

Shelly and Gregg already knew they faced a much more challenging future. We wanted to be there for them any way we could.

During my recovery several cancer support groups had contacted me to offer their unique help and compassionate understanding. I found great value in this. Shelly did, too. We clearly need one another.

Her oncologist prescribed an aggressive course of chemotherapy and radiation treatments. At the time, reconstructive plastic surgery was not an option for her.

She was so self-conscious about her missing breast she couldn't even undress in front of her husband yet. What agony. She wore her regular bras and just put a zip-lock bag filled with Minute Rice in the cup where her breast once was. I could definitely relate.

On the day I was cleared to drive, Shelly called me. Her doctor had ordered a customized prosthetic breast and she had been notified that it was finally ready to be picked up. However, Shelly was not yet cleared to drive and Gregg was on a business trip…so I picked her up and we were off to pick up her new breast together.

Goodbye, Minute Rice. From now on we'll just serve it with dinner!

When we arrived at the medical supply center neither one of us had the strength to open their heavy glass front door. So we just stood there. Then we laughed at our dilemma. Finally, because I had logged a bit more post-op recovery time, I took a shot at opening the door. I managed to pry it open just enough to squeeze my foot into the crevice and use my leg to open it the rest of the way. In we marched, triumphantly.

Once inside, Shelly and I suggested the medical supply center consider installing a door that would be more easily accessible to "amputees" like us! Again, we started to giggle. Humor is a great stress-reliever sometimes.

Shelly's order was brought to her for her to "try on." She asked me to come into the dressing room to assist her. She intentionally revealed her body. This was a great honor for me. She trusted me and it was my utmost privilege to be the first to encourage her over this difficult and deeply emotional hurdle.

The prosthesis was perfect and I could sense her relief and delight. She took a significant step toward personal restitution and I was blessed by her bravery.

I excused myself and waited in the reception area as Shelly got dressed and went to the counter to pay for her order…only to discover that she had forgotten to bring her purse since she wasn't driving. She did not have her wallet, credit cards or her checkbook. So I wrote the check and purchased her brand new breast for her. We both laughed out loud again! The receptionist seemed to truly understand our gleefulness and our much-needed levity, and we appreciated her kindness and helpfulness.

As we drove home, at one point there was a speed bump in the road. I slowly drove over the bump and both Shelly's and my new breasts actually jiggled a bit. "Wheeeee," we both spontaneously exclaimed! We shared one more little step toward normality.

It turned into a pretty enjoyable road trip, my first time back behind the wheel. Under the circumstances.

CHAPTER TWENTY-THREE

The Common Denominator

I thought about my time with Shelly that day. I prayed for her and for her family. Shelly also had young daughters. I knew she was deeply burdened by the same concern for them that I had for Sarah and Amy, although neither one of us verbalized it. We just couldn't. Some breast cancer is hereditary. Thankfully, it is not always passed on. I knew she gleaned some hope from that and prayed for her daughters to be protected from the dreadful disease, as I did for mine.

I thought about the chuckles Shelly and I had shared that afternoon as well. I was thankful we could just go ahead and enjoy some enthusiastic, healing laughter. Obviously, we both understood that there's certainly nothing comical about cancer, but sometimes crying and laughing provide precisely the same cathartic release.

I thought about Shelly's courageous revelation of her body to me and I was reminded of the nurse who "flashed me" in the office. And my friend's mother who revealed her newly reconstructed breasts to me before she had even put down her purse. Our individual situations were as unique as we were, but each of us experienced the identical need to "test drive" our new status as prosthetic-recipients. I prayed that we would all be able to cherish the gifts of our post-surgical bodies.

I thought about Shelly's going to pick up her prosthesis, yet completely forgetting to bring any means of paying for it. I thought about similar stories other women, virtual strangers, had openly shared with me as we passed the time in various medical waiting rooms along the way. I thought about all the manifestations of my own unfamiliar post-surgical/recovery behavior.

Although we each spoke of these occurrences with smiles on our faces, deep down we were all baffled and troubled by them. I prayed that we would not condemn ourselves for our temporarily absent-minded, out-of-character, rather bizarre and otherwise unsettling post-surgical behavior. This too shall pass.

I prayed that we would be able to extend grace to others as well. Like the people who blatantly stare at your chest once they've learned of your situation…or the people who think they've *discreetly* glanced at your chest (we see you, by the way), upon learning you've undergone mastectomies. Albeit, there is a natural curiosity, but when you're already dealing with insecurities of such colossal magnitude, the stares really hurt.

Then I prayed to be free of the guilt I carried about my having pre-cancerous cells and not the precarious late-stage malignancy Shelly and so many other women I knew currently faced. Then I forgave myself for having tumors in the first place.

And I forgave God.

CHAPTER TWENTY-FOUR

Me And "My Buddy"

My strength and stamina were gradually increasing and since I was now able to drive, I was excited to be able to attend a special conference being held at our church. I must admit that I was also a bit tentative as this was my first solo outing.

The featured speaker was a renowned and respected Christian author/speaker whom I had admired for years. His unique insights combined with his exceptional ability to communicate God's Word from a practical and distinct viewpoint are outstanding. I grasped the Truth of my identity in Christ as a result of his teaching.

I wisely allotted plenty of extra travel time since I was still only able to move at a snail's pace. Plus, I was still carrying my pillow, "My Buddy," with me at all times; I had some definite logistic challenges to account for.

I was somewhat early for the conference and "just happened" to reach the door of our church at the precise moment the keynote speaker arrived. My friend, Beth, who served on the ministry team responsible for coordinating the event, had the privilege of meeting his airplane, and she was in the process of escorting him into the building. I was thrilled when Beth introduced us and we exchanged pleasant greetings. Beth noticed the pillow (it was pretty obvious!) and naturally recognized the pillowcase covering "My Buddy." She made a brief comment to me about it, we all smiled and there was a bit of I've-read-all-of-your-books-so-honored-to-have-met-you-type conversation, and I turned to make my way into the auditorium to secure a seat.

But he did not let me go at that. He picked right up on Beth's comment and asked her about me. She briefly explained to him and happened to mention that this was my first time back to church since the Sunday before my surgery.

I kid you not; he loped down the hall after me, leaving Beth in his dust. He very gently took my arm, looked me right in the eyes and sincerely thanked me for making the effort to come to hear him that morning. He told me Beth had shared my circumstances with him and he would be in prayer for me. I was astounded.

Then, he asked me point-blank "What is your greatest fear?"

What popped out of my mouth was a whopper! I heard myself pipe up with, "I'm afraid my husband will leave me for a woman who has nipples."

Where is that escape-hatch in the floor when you need it? I wanted to crawl back to my car and get out of there! Where on earth had that come from? Was I losing my mind? I was completely mortified to have said such a thing.

Not to mention the fact that Bill would NEVER do anything like that!

Without missing a beat, this godly gentleman put his arm around my shoulder and thanked me profusely for my honest answer to his question. He told me he could "hear the agony in my voice" and now better understood how to pray for me, which is precisely why he asked the question in the first place. With his arm still around me and my arms holding "My Buddy," he walked me up and down the hall and even into the kitchen as he prayed for me.

He spoke a blessing over me. He prayed against the enemy's tempting me with the shattering fear I had just expressed. His prayer seemed to go on forever…touching every single issue I had hidden in my heart. I was set free. What a profoundly Spirit-filled moment we shared!

He made ME a priority. He focused completely on MY need. The conference was delayed a few more minutes and that was fine with him. At that moment, he was serving ME on behalf of my Father. He had followed God's prompting to our Divine appointment. He was genuine and humble and completely oblivious to the on-lookers and those in charge of the conference. For that brief moment his heart was locked with mine in communion with the Holy Spirit.

To be totally honest, during the conference my mind drifted to the enormity of my pre-conference experience with our distinguished speaker. I will never, ever forget my encounter with him. To me, his "actions" spoke far louder than the "words" of his presentation that day. He had manifested Christ to me. May God bless you, Dr. Bill Gillham.

And thank you, Jesus, for wrapping your ever-loving, ever-present arms around me and upholding me with Your righteous right hand. Thank you for completely removing that deep, ugly, fear-packed lie and replacing it with a cherished experience of Your grace and compassion. Glory to Your Holy Name.

CHAPTER TWENTY-FIVE

Oh No, Not You Again!

Unfortunately, the ripples of this loathsome lake continued to spread wider still. My friend Shelly's sister was motivated to check her breasts once she learned of Shelly's breast cancer. Sure enough, she also discovered an abnormal protuberance. Diagnosis: stage four malignancy. Surgery and chemotherapy followed.

My friend Linda's sister called me after she detected a bulky nodule in her breast. Diagnosis: malignancy. Surgery and chemotherapy for her as well.

After her sister's cancer was revealed, my cherished friend Linda underwent testing herself. Tumor discovered. Diagnosis: malignancy. Surgery and chemotherapy for Linda.

Same abhorrent scenario over and over and over again.

Breast cancer has literally reached epidemic levels. The good news is, and I believe there is always "good" as described in Romans 8, as awareness and incidents continue to increase, research has advanced and noteworthy discoveries have been made.

And continue to be made every day. EVERY day. Diagnostic techniques, superior medications, successful treatments and improved courses of therapy. Combined with support groups. Communication. And hope. There is a lot of good news.

Still, there is always the lingering "elephant in the room." And, yes, that's also a "good" thing. However, we must fight the urge to obsess over it. Kept in balance, the "elephant" can actually become our friend.

Five years after my breast tumors were detected and destroyed, during my regular annual gynecological check-up, "something" was discovered in my uterus. No symptoms, nothing unusual, just a routine exam and then...

"I'd like you to go, right now, for an ultrasound," my doctor said, "Although I don't think it's anything to be alarmed about at this point."

Okay. Sure. Nothing to be alarmed about…just routine… not impressive…I repeated that mantra as I carried my orders to the next office complex and underwent the "routine" ultrasound. Not impressive. Just routine. Except for the very silent technician, who broke her silence only to say, "Mrs. Weaver, after you dress why don't you stop back by your doctor's office. I'll give him a call to let him know you're on your way." "Now?" "Yes." This time I boldly asked, "You found something didn't you?" Unbelievably, she actually answered. "Yes. There is a grapefruit-sized tumor in your uterus."

Here we go again. This time Bill and I faced a much shorter sequence of apprehension and concern. As soon as we could get things scheduled, my doctor performed a total hysterectomy and, unfortunately, because of their "involvement" I lost both of my ovaries as well. This immediately thrust me into menopause.

The pathology report of these tumors described findings remarkably similar to the composition of my breast tumors. PRE-cancerous cells. God's merciful timing was perfect once again. How could I deny His hand? How could this be anything but another miracle? I had absolutely no indication of a problem, yet God knew there were abnormalities and He intervened in time to prevent disaster. Again!

And, again, I experienced the extraordinary compassion and generosity of my family as well as my Christian family during my post-surgical recovery process. Vickie drove over two hours to deliver a still-warm, home-cooked dinner to us. A wonderful meal that included applesauce she had made herself, from organic apples she had picked herself, because she knew apples were helpful in the fight against cancer.

One note, one word of encouragement, one intercessory prayer, one phone call, one pan of brownies may not seem like enormously significant gestures in themselves, but *most definitely* they are! Thoughtful, compassionate and kind, they are literally lifelines!

"Like apples of gold in settings of silver is a word spoken in right circumstances." (Proverbs 25:11[NASB])

For the second time, my PRE-cancerous tumors required no chemotherapy. I began hormone replacement therapy, which is no picnic let me tell you, but certainly nothing like chemotherapy.

My doctor prescribed various hormones in various strengths in an effort to determine the right "cocktail" for me. I felt like Goldilocks. This one's too strong; this one's too weak. I was boiling hot and bloated all the time. Or I was freezing cold. I was up all night or I was falling on my face. But one symptom was worse than all the others combined.

Bill unsuspectingly came happily home from work one day and I barked at him that, "I had now been cursed with DOG hearing!" Having learned the hard way to tread *very* lightly these days, he quietly asked what I meant. Like that was a normal comment. Dog hearing.

"I can hear EVERYTHING. Sounds humans don't normally hear…sounds only dogs can hear. It's driving me CRAZY. I can hear our neighbor vacuuming two houses down the street!"

Bill's gentleness and patience, combined with the doctor's perseverance at finding the right cocktail, eventually reaped the desired result. What a relief.

In God's time, I recovered from the surgery, grew in strength and stability and life as we remembered it resumed.

NOTE: Hormone Replacement Therapy is a somewhat controversial treatment for some patients. Mine was prescribed after much prayer, research, discussion, testing and consultation. Always, always glean as much information as you can and certainly communicate honestly with your doctor.

CHAPTER TWENTY-SIX

Baby Oil and Iodine

I am a product of the sun-worshipping sixties! Cybill Shepherd and Cheryl Tiegs wearing madras two-piece bathing suits and matching triangle scarves on the cover of *Seventeen* Magazine. Blonde and tan. That was the ultimate look to strive for.

Well, I was blonde, but I was NEVER tan. As hard as I tried, my pattern was painful red sunburn followed by peeling, flaky skin.

My best friend, Linda, and I spent many an hour on the beach working on our tans. Baking in the hot sun, slathering on the homemade, tried-and-true suntan concoction of one-part baby oil mixed with one-part iodine. Then we'd time ourselves…always following the pattern of the sun. Flipping and moving to maximize exposure and "catch some rays." Constantly comparing limbs to determine which of us was getting darker sooner.

With auburn brown hair, Linda would invariably come away with smooth, latte-colored, beautifully tanned skin.

I looked more like a swollen lobster, but was quite proud of my accomplishment as well.

Then we'd douse ourselves in "Après le Sole" crème and repeat the routine the following day. From time to time we also utilized the pleated silver "reflectors" which directed more sun onto our bodies to speed up and increase our "tans." I don't even want to discuss our use of sun lamps, which supplemented our beach activities.

Even now I can hear my mother's voice constantly warning me against using a sun lamp! Why didn't I listen?

Bill is a typical manly-man. It's like pulling teeth to get him to go to the doctor. He discovered a little "spot" on his ankle and made the fatal mistake of mentioning it to me. Well, I reacted like the typical wife. Bugged him constantly to see a doctor, to no avail.

One day I happened to read in the newspaper that a Health Fair was being conducted at our local shopping mall. Bill came home from work to find Sarah, Amy and me standing with our purses over our arms, in the driveway, blocking the garage doors. "We're going to the mall," I stated. As a community service, various free medical tests were offered and I knew a dermatologist would be offering his professional services as well. So off we four went to the mall.

First stop, Bill to the dermatologist. As I was waiting for Bill, the volunteer asked if I'd like to be seen next. I told her I hadn't planned to be seen. "It's free," she said. Okay, I thought. Why not?

Bill emerged from his examination and was happy to report that his "spot" was perfectly fine. Thank you, Jesus! We were so grateful!

My turn. As I sat in the examination chair, the doctor took one look at my face and pointed his finger saying, "That's malignant, and that's malignant and that's malignant." What did he just say? Did I just hear the "m" word? There was talk of follow-up appointments, but I don't remember much else. Except that I was sent over to the blood-pressure station next.

The technician took my pressure and repeated the test twice before he said, "Ma'am your blood pressure is dangerously high." Still in shock, I said, "Oh, it's fine. I just found out I have skin cancer. Give me a minute to settle down and I'm sure it will go back to normal." Poor guy was visibly relieved.

As it turned out, at the completion of the week long Health Fair, I was the only person on whom skin cancer was detected. I certainly didn't suspect I had skin cancer. I never even noticed the places that were so obvious to the dermatologist. Having skin cancer never even occurred to me. We went to the Health Fair for Bill's sake, but Jesus knew it was my face that was of concern; my health that was AGAIN in jeopardy. Incredibly, AGAIN, Jesus was protecting me. AGAIN, preempting potential disaster.

I made an appointment with a dermatologist Bill had gone to high school with, but had lost touch with over the many intervening years. The local television station, which was a co-sponsor of the Health Fair, called me one day to ask if they could "follow my case" to encourage others to attend subsequent Health Fairs and follow-up with their doctors. I said, "As long as you allow me to say everything I want to say, including giving glory to God, I'll allow full access to my records and be filmed and interviewed as you wish." They agreed.

I met the reporter and photographer at the doctor's office and I could see people glancing at us, trying to figure out who I was. They filmed me entering the reception area, in the waiting room, speaking with the nurse, meeting with the doctor. I had to laugh at the curious reaction of the other patients. I wondered if any of the nurses who tended me during my mastectomies would see this broadcast!

I was able to ask all the questions and make all the comments I wanted to, and the segment aired with little editing of my remarks.

After subsequent visits Bill's friend, the dermatologist, operated to remove a cancerous tumor from my face, just under my nose and above my lip.

Praise God, although it was quite large subcutaneously, the tumor was not a melanoma, but a far less invasive basal cell carcinoma. Left undetected, growing, its roots would have invaded my jawbone and would have required his removing my tongue, jawbone and teeth. There is a scar on my face, but he operated with such skill and care the scar is now almost unnoticeable.

I've had five more basal cell carcinomas removed from my face, and I'm told there will be more surgery to come. These are direct results of my numerous sunburns in my endless quest for the perfect tan.

I've learned a great deal about skin cancer from Bill's friend and from the research I have also conducted on my own. God has granted me opportunities to share what I've learned and in the process I've been afforded opportunities to witness to His providential care. All because of my experience with a skin cancer discovery at the Health Fair.

I've written newsletter articles. I've spoken at women's church groups. I've lectured at the girls' schools. I shared my faith with Bill's friend, the dermatologist. I even shared with a woman in the grocery store. She had seen the television segment and recognized me! She asked me to check a place on her hand that she was concerned about.

I told her I was just a layperson and she should see her doctor for professional advice, but I was able to share with her about the "professional" I knew best, Jesus Christ. He allowed me those unique and wonderful opportunities to share about Him and I feel blessed and thankful that He turned my skin cancer into "good" in that way.

Unfortunately, skin cancer is also at epidemic proportions now. And it doesn't just wreak minor complications. Our dear friend, Dean, valiantly battled melanoma to the very moment Jesus called him home.

Yet there continue to be informative "weapons" to help us each battle skin cancer. Take heed. You've no doubt heard and read the admonitions to limit exposure to the sun, which is the most dangerous skin cancer risk factor. Always use sunscreen with high SPF's (sun protection factor) and check to be sure the product's effectiveness has not expired. Expiration dates are displayed on the packaging.

I'll bet you've also heard these warnings: don't use sun lamps or utilize tanning beds, no matter how much you're told they're safe.

Listen to your mothers. They're right.

CHAPTER TWENTY-SEVEN

Diffuse!

One of my favorite luxuries is a leisurely bubble bath. Even as a little girl, I loved them.

One afternoon while Bill was at work and the girls in high school, I decided to indulge myself in the superb splendor of a bubble bath. However, for some unknown reason, I drew the bath in the girls' bathroom instead of the master bath. I have no idea why I chose their room, but I do recall that I couldn't wait to dim the lights and immerse myself into the magnificent, pastel-tinted, floral-scented lavish bubbles. Ahhhh. Peace and quiet. THIS was my idea of total relaxation.

Completely engulfed in sumptuous pleasure, I folded my arms behind my head to cushion my neck as I slipped down deeper into the warm, fragrant water. Because Sarah and Amy's bathtub was in the "reverse" position from the one in the master bath, my arms must have folded into an unusual position or something. I'm not exactly sure what transpired. Anyway, in the middle of my moment of pampered delight, I was somehow suddenly thrust into an awkwardly-arm-flailing process of preventing myself from drowning in a treacherous sea of bubble-filled water. It was quite strange. Then, as I attempted to position myself more comfortably, I somehow pressed up against a soap dish or something and felt that unmistakable "ole' feeling" again. With a start, I sat right up. I checked one more time. Definitely. There it was. An abnormal, irregular bulge in my left armpit. Felt it with my fingers, felt it pressing inward again. I gasped for breath as chills shot up and down my spine.

So much for my spa escape in the middle of the afternoon.

It had been years since my mastectomies and hysterectomy. During that time I had been regularly performing self-exams, visiting both my breast doctor and my gynecologist. I faithfully underwent all the required tests and all reports had been good, all systems "go." How could this be? How can I face this again? I just can't. No, no, no...

But we did face it again. Together. Step by step again. And this time my breast doctor also referred me to a very high-ranking specialist, an oncologist, for even further testing.

There was a palpable gravity about the specialist's office. Even his office waiting room, which was immaculately clean, decorated, but not welcoming, communicated, "This is serious."

The receptionist was pleasant, but not overly friendly. The appointments were conducted precisely on time. The other patients in the waiting room were much quieter, much more somber than those I had ever been with before. The entire atmosphere in this office was distinctly different from anything I had previously experienced.

Just before I was to enter the examination room, I heard the nurse speaking over the telephone with someone at the hospital where I had had all of my surgeries. She requested a compilation of my medical history. She asked that all of my records and reports be Faxed to her immediately. I thought to myself, good luck getting that! I had barely completed the thought before her Fax machine started flipping and flying! Wow. That was impressive. This doctor obviously carried significant clout.

Like the receptionist, the specialist was pleasant, but not friendly. He commanded respect. He examined me, felt for the mass; confirmed its presence. He wanted to check me again in a month.

During the return visit, he again felt the mass. By now I was undone. This doctor did not mince words. Straight as an arrow, this guy. "There is a mass in your remaining lymph node." I could feel myself getting teary. He had absolutely no tolerance for that. I recall comments like, "Well, what do you expect? It's a lymph node; it's clearing imperfections from your system. It's performing as it is supposed to." With my heart pounding, tears welling, voice trembling, I managed to say something about fearing lymphoma and was cancer developing in my last lymph node?

Almost irritated, he firmly stated, "You didn't have cancer, you had PRE-cancerous tumors." Then, in the most graphic animation of a point I've ever seen a doctor display, he flailed his arms above his head and literally shouted, "Diffuse! Diffuse! Your body is performing precisely as it should."

I told him about my episodes of skin cancer. And he calmed those fears as well.

His voice was quieter, but his next statement lives in my ears and memory. I'll quote it, verbatim, forever, I'm sure. "Your body has a propensity to the disease of cancer." Thankfully, he followed that statement with, "The mass in your lymph node, your previous tumors and your skin cancer all originate from different sources. Go home. Diffuse. You're fine."

So, with great drama, I was exhorted to DIFFUSE, but to balance that with the "elephant in the room." To maintain a course of vigilant personal observation combined with regular medical check-ups by my breast specialist, gynecologist and dermatologist.

Bottom line:
Be wise, but don't freak out.

CHAPTER TWENTY-EIGHT

To Be
Perfectly Honest

If it were up to me, I would never have chosen my experiences with cancer. That's an obvious statement. Or so I thought.

Recently a supposedly well-meaning Christian friend abruptly confronted me saying, "What's all this cancer about? What sin in your life continues to result in cancer?" I was blind-sided by her crude question, but eventually I became grateful for it. It inspired me to search my heart for any unconfessed sin.

But, in response to her confrontation, let me just state (as I did to her) that while there is some correlation between sin and sickness, I do not believe we bring cancer upon ourselves. Nor do I believe Jesus brings cancer into our lives as a punishment for sin. He DIED for our sins. We were set free. We live under grace. We are healed by His stripes. His Name is Jehovah Rapha, The God Who HEALS. (Psalm 103:3)

It will be wonderful when the disease is completely eradicated. I firmly believe one day it will be.

Yet death is a part of life. The fact of the matter, of course, is that cancer is still a factor and we must contend with it, utilizing every weapon the medical and spiritual arsenals afford us. And, those are significant weapons to be sure! Every detail, every piece of research, each new medical discovery, every pink ribbon and every step "walked"... are under HIS control.

I, for one, choose to trust God's Word and dwell on what I have learned during this journey. Each day I have learned to trust Him more.

And, although I did not choose my adventure with cancer, I would not trade one single moment of it. The worst experience has been the greatest gift I have ever received. Sound like an oxymoron? Perhaps I should explain what I mean.

I have never been more helpless, yet secure in Him; never been more vulnerable, yet so completely safe; never been more out of control of my circumstances; yet never been more "connected" with Him. As Bill and I committed each step of this journey to Him, we were granted the peace that passes understanding. We absolutely and undeniably experienced one promise from His Word after another fulfilled and become tangible realities in our lives. I literally sat in Jesus' lap; safely enfolded in His mighty and tender loving arms. I will never forget the power of that indescribable peace. Perfect peace.

So take heart. His plans are always for good and not evil to those who love Him and are called according to His purpose. We are blessed.

All praise to our loving omniscient and omnipotent God! Know Him, Trust Him, Dwell in Perfect Peace.

"Thou dost keep him (her) in perfect peace whose mind is stayed on Thee, because he (she) trusts in Thee." (Isaiah 26:3^{KJV})

CHAPTER TWENTY-NINE

Now What?

"Perfectly, wonderfully, normal." That's a direct quote from my breast specialist following my most recent annual examination.

I'll admit that I've expressed some concern over the years regarding my having silicone implants, particularly in light of the reports and media attention that flare up from time to time. Consistently, he has dissuaded my concern, encouraging me to focus only on facts, not "fads." Reminding me that I'm among the fortunate women to have had the opportunity of having this option, which is no longer available. (Saline solution is now used in place of silicone gel.)

At the time of this writing almost twenty years have passed since my mastectomies and fifteen since my hysterectomy. I've continued to have basal cell carcinomas removed from my face and ear lobes, but have not had to face melanoma. I've enjoyed good health and great happiness. "Perfectly, wonderfully, normal!"

Shelly moved away and we've lost touch, but last I heard both she and her sister were well. Barbara and Jill are both completely well. And, happily, Linda and her sister, as well as their mother, are all perfectly healthy, strong and cancer-free following their surgeries and treatments.

Even so, can any of us completely eliminate the thought of recurring cancer? I don't believe we can. I don't think that makes us unwise or spiritually untrusting. Cancer has been our reality. And that elephant is still eating peanuts.

Four years ago "abnormal cells" were found during my routine gynecological exam. More tests followed. More procedures were conducted. I'll spare you the graphic details.

The bottom line: I was diagnosed with a form of cervical cancer. Since I have already undergone a complete hysterectomy/oopharectomy, my treatment options are uniquely limited. I utilize chemotherapy cream and have undergone several surgical procedures to remove cancerous cells, layer by layer. For now, I am perfectly well and my doctor is keeping a watchful eye. I continue the therapy and measures currently available to me and all is well. My God is in control.

And my heart is truly at peace. It really is. My hope is in Him. My life is in Him. Just as I sang that Sunday morning, so many years ago. And great has been Thy faithfulness, Lord, unto me!

CHAPTER THIRTY

I Learned This One The Hard Way

Breast cancer has now reached epidemic levels. I'd venture to say that if you're reading this, either you yourself or someone you know has been impacted by this disease.

Ironically, several years before my mastectomies one of my friends, who had moved to another state, called me one day to inform me that her former neighbor (whom I had met a few times casually) had been diagnosed with aggressive late-stage breast cancer. My friend asked if I would go to her neighbor and share Christ with her. I told her I would.

But in those days the thought of "sharing Christ" with a woman I barely knew completely terrified me. I felt inadequate and convinced myself that this was way beyond what I was capable of. I prayed for her but I procrastinated, paralyzed by fear, and put off calling her or asking if I could visit with her.

Her cancer progressed rapidly and her condition soon became extremely critical. I sat down and wrote her a lengthy note…sharing my faith, sharing the plan of salvation, sharing the fact that my friend had asked me to contact her, sharing the fact that I'd been praying for her and I said I'd come see her if she would like for me to do so. Then I mailed the note.

A few days later I received a telephone call from the woman's mother-in-law. She thanked me; saying my note had arrived, but tragically, not in time for her daughter-in-law to read for she had passed away the previous week. I could hardly breathe, but managed to express my condolences. When I hung up the phone I was shocked, sad and ashamed and I wept to my very core.

Did she EVER hear the plan of salvation? Did she KNOW how much Jesus loved her and that He died for her? Did she EVER have the opportunity of praying to ask forgiveness of her sins and receiving Christ into her life? Did my cowardice prevent her from spending eternity with Him?

I failed to fulfill my promise to my friend and only Jesus knows how that affected her former neighbor's salvation. Although I asked for forgiveness, I learned the hard way that the pain of my failure far surpassed any trepidation I may have had at the time.

I do not ever want to miss another opportunity to share the love of Christ. Thankfully, my experience with cancer during these nearly twenty years has afforded me many,

many opportunities to do just that, and I am truly grateful for this profound privilege.

Perhaps today you face an uncertain future. May I ask you to consider yourself to be the neighbor I never spoke with?

Whatever your need at the moment, know that God loves you and you can place your hope and trust in Him. Cast all your concerns upon Him, for He cares for you and He will never fail you or forsake you. (Joshua 1:5[NASB])

He wants to give you a future and a hope.

"For I know the plans that I have for you, 'declares the Lord,' plans for good and not evil to give you a future and a hope." (Jeremiah 29:11)

"For God so loved the world, that He gave His only begotten Son, that whoever believes in Him should not perish, but have everlasting life. For God did not send His Son into the world to condemn the world, but that the world through Him might be saved." (John 3:16-17[NKJV])

Saved from what??? From the punishment for sin. Perhaps you hadn't considered yourself a sinner, but the Bible says in Romans 3:23 that *"ALL have sinned, and fall short of the glory of God."* And the "wages" or punishment for sin is "death" or spiritual separation from God. (Romans 6:23) Jesus came to change that.

God loves you! He does not want sin to separate you from Him. *"But God demonstrates His own love toward us, in that while we were yet sinners, Christ died for us."* (Rom.5:8[NASB]) *"...Fixing our eyes on Jesus, the author and perfecter of faith, Who FOR THE JOY set before Him endured the cross, despising the shame..."* (Hebrews 12:2[NASB]) God sent Jesus to pay the punishment for our sin so we won't have to. He loves us that much. He loves YOU that much. It was the JOY of the relationship with YOU that was set before Him.

Receive His love. *"Yet to all who receive Him, to those who believe in His Name, He gave the right to become children of God."* (John 1:12). The choice is yours. Will you place your faith in Jesus? Faith is not just believing facts about Jesus, faith is trusting in Jesus. *"For everyone who calls on the name of the Lord will be saved."* (Romans 10:13)

Are you willing to place your faith in Jesus right now? You can simply turn AWAY from sin and TO God through Jesus. This is repentance...not just feeling sorry for your sin, but turning from it. *"Repent, then, and turn to God, so that your sins may be wiped out."* (Acts 3:19)

Just call on Jesus and He will become your personal Savior and Lord. This is God's gift to you. *"For it is by grace you have been saved, through faith – and this not from yourselves, it is the gift of God."* (Ephesians 2:8)

How do you call on Jesus? Through prayer, which is simply talking with God. You can pray the following prayer, or use similar words of your own; Jesus WILL become your Savior and you will be His forever. *"If you confess with your mouth the Lord Jesus and believe in your heart that God has raised Him from the dead, you WILL be saved."* (Romans 10:9)

You can receive Jesus Christ through prayer, RIGHT NOW! If the following prayer expresses the desire of your heart, you can say the following prayer out loud or silently and Jesus WILL come into your life just as He promised:

"Dear God, I know that Jesus is Your Son and that He died on the cross and was raised from the dead. I know I have sinned and need forgiveness and Jesus died on the cross for that very reason. I want to turn from my sins and receive Jesus as my personal Savior and Lord. I invite You to come into my life and help me live in a way that brings You joy. I pray this in Jesus' Name, Amen."

Now rest in His tender arms of grace and let His peace fill your heart. You need to pray this prayer only one time in your life because Jesus promised, in Hebrews 13:5b[NKJV] that He will *"never leave you nor forsake you."*

Praise God!

CHAPTER THIRTY-ONE

When You Least Expect It

I had come to terms with my health situation. After all, it had been years since my mastectomies and hysterectomy. The basal cell carcinomas seemed fairly manageable as long as I maintained routine check-ups with the dermatologist. The cervical cancer situation was under control and physically, overall, I felt perfectly well.

As strange as this may sound, with all of my heart I consider my health journey to be a profound GIFT from God. Psalm 119:71[NASB] says, "*It is GOOD for me that I was afflicted, that I may learn Thy statutes.*" As a result of the experiences I've shared in this book, and many I have not, I know, deep in my soul, how completely God loves me and was reminded over and over and over again of His intimate care and concern for me. I learned in tangible ways that nothing can separate me from the love of God. Not even cancer or pre-cancer.

I've been afforded countless opportunities to encourage other women to "*consider it all joy*" (James 1:2[NASB]) when they face the challenge of breast cancer. And I was profoundly touched when the women in a neighborhood Bible Study I was leading unexpectedly blessed me by making a donation, in my name, to further breast cancer research. So many, many women had helped me negotiate my way through the mire of breast cancer and now, because of the generosity of my dear friends, others would be helped "in my name."

I felt as though the healing circle had been completed... a tangible demonstration of 2 Corinthians 1:3[NASB]:

"Blessed be the God and Father of our Lord Jesus Christ, the Father of mercies and God of all comfort; Who comforts us in all our affliction so that we may be able to comfort those who are in any affliction with the comfort with which we, ourselves, are comforted by God."

All the pain was behind me. Until the day I filled out the form.

I don't remember what the purpose was, but I was filling the blanks on a routine application form for something...name, address, state. I came to the box that asked me to check "male" or "female" and I completely fell apart. I was absolutely distraught. I cried and cried and thought to myself, "I have no more female parts...no breasts, no nipples, no uterus, no ovaries...there is no category for me on this form!" I am not a female any longer...what AM I? Where do I belong? I don't have a category! I was shocked at the depth of my emotional agony and profound sense of loss.

Bill helped me to see that I was believing a lie. And that lie had tainted my feelings about myself and produced harmful actions. Bill exhorted me to focus on TRUTH so I would be set free from the enemy's trap.

Bill assured me I still was and always will be a woman. He prayed with me and helped me to recall the verses that describe who God says I am:

Complete and perfect (Colossians 2:10)
Totally accepted (Ephesians. 1:6)
Redeemed and justified (Romans. 3:24)
A child of God (Romans. 8:16-17)
FREE from the law of sin and death (Romans. 8:2)
Free to confidently access God (Ephesians. 3:12)
Blessed (Ephesians. 1:3)
Set apart/sanctified (1 Corinthians 1:2)
I am the righteousness of God (2 Corinthians 5:2)
Loved by God (Jeremiah 31:3)
He has called ME by name, and I am His (Isaiah 43:1)
He created me FEMALE (Genesis 1:27)

I am a precious daughter of God and that will forever be my "category." I have learned, in no uncertain terms, that I am free to live a happy, complete and victorious life here on earth, and I've embraced the reality of what my doctor once told me, **"You don't need nipples to get into heaven."**

Take joy, my King! Amen!

At the very least

Please make every effort to pay attention to your breasts. I don't mean fitting them into a pretty lacy bra and wearing a fancy top…I mean pay ATTENTION to them.

At the very least you need to perform self-examination of your breasts every month. Every month. When you take your morning shower or evening bubble bath (hey, a girl can dream can't she?) take a moment and familiarize yourself with your breasts. While you're still wet and with your eyes closed.

Then, take a look at yourself in the mirror before you get dressed. Notice any skin puckering or discharge. Notice any tiny finger-like protrusions. Notice any bulges or unusual shape. Are both sides fairly uniform in size?

Sadly, statistics prove that EVERY woman is at risk for breast cancer. Don't let fear keep you from taking this seriously.

If you DO feel something or see something, get to the doctor immediately! Don't do what I did…early detection is the key to the cure. Nearly 98% of breast cancer is curable if detected early enough.

145

Get yourself a breast buddy. Someone, like Kitty, who loves you enough to hold you accountable for regular breast self-examination; someone for whom you can return the favor.

How To Examine Your Breasts

Be aware of how your breasts normally look and feel and check them regularly! It's best to check your breasts when they're not tender or swollen. Note: A firm ridge in the lower curve of each breast is normal.

Lie down flat and place your RIGHT arm behind your head. Using the tips of your three middle fingers on your LEFT hand, feel for lumps in your right breast. Use circular motions to feel the breast tissue of your entire breast. (If you're not sure how firmly to press, ask your doctor or nurse to show you.)

Next move around your breast in and up and down pattern starting at an imaginary line drawn straight down your side from your underarm to your sternum (chest bone). Be sure to check both sides of the imaginary line.

REPEAT this process on your LEFT breast with your left arm behind your head, using the three middle fingers on your RIGHT hand to feel your left breast.

Now STAND in front of a mirror with your arms straight at your side, hands pressing firmly down onto your hips. Look at your breasts for any changes in size, shape, contour, dimpling, pulling or redness or scaliness of the nipple or breast skin.

Then raise your arms straight above your head, pressing your palms together, and check in the mirror for the same things.

Relax your arms. Use your left hand to check for any lumps in your right armpit. Then use your right hand to check your left armpit.

While breast self-examination is certainly important, the other methods of maintaining breast health are also critical.

Regular breast exams by your doctor and scheduled mammograms combined with your own careful observations may literally save your life.

I Wish Someone Would Have Told Me This

It's a proven fact that early detection saves lives. But remember, finding a breast change does not necessarily mean there is cancer! If you DO discover a change in your breast, see your doctor immediately. If you DO face breast cancer:

Don't go to doctor appointments alone. Someone else needs to serve as your advocate; to listen to the doctor, to listen for the explanation of the pathology and/or lab reports, to listen carefully to follow-up instructions, etc.

Do your own research. This does not mean the RESPONSIBILITY for your own treatment is yours... absolutely not...but the more informed you are, the better your treatment will be. You and your doctor and staff are a TEAM...a team whose goal is the best possible care and treatment of the "star"...that's you!

Set up a notebook. Begin with the very first appointment with your doctor and then keep your notebook handy... write down the questions you want to ask your doctor and then write down the answers (or have your advocate write them down). Keep your notebook by the phone so you can write down any information that is passed along to you via the telephone. Keep pamphlets and various materials you gather in the notebook.

Use it as your reference file. Add a section to be your journal…write your feelings and keep written records of all your victories…keep encouraging notes and verses and personal messages in it. Read your journal in waiting rooms.

Keep your mind focused and fixed on God's Truth. Let your journal serve as an encouraging "Joshua stone" for you. (Joshua, Chapter 24)

Don't isolate yourself. Even though there will be times when that's precisely what you'll want to do. Sometimes the last thing you feel like doing is talking. Okay, so don't talk. But let someone else talk. Or just be quiet together. I urge you to let others minister to you…if it's too hard for you to "receive," remember that others NEED to demonstrate God's love to you just as much as you need to receive it. Plus, it's empowering to YOU to allow God to bless them by serving you. Don't rob them, or yourself, of the blessing.

Give yourself a break. Sometimes you'll just feel angry… even angry with God. He understands. You can be honest, but be careful. Don't give the enemy a foothold to spiral you down into fear and resentment and sin. Don't wallow in negativity. Give yourself five minutes to be upset if you need to, and then TURN from it. (Literally set the kitchen timer for five minutes...and then STOP!) Put on some praise music...sometimes it's even too hard to read the Word. During those moments, let the uplifting sounds of worship immerse you in His presence. He inhabits the praises of His people. Relax, rest and commune with Him.

Focus on Truth. He gave us all of our senses. And He speaks to us through them. Taste His goodness in whatever you eat, especially in the food people share with you; See Him in the sunrise or the rain or a flower or even a weed; Feel His power in the wind or His gentleness in a cool breeze or a warm bath; Hear His voice in the laughter of a child or a bird's song or carried in the voice of a loving friend. (Philippians 4:8)

After your surgery you will be exhausted. However, you will probably be on the receiving end of many phone calls from family and friends offering support and prayer. As uplifting as these calls are, it's sometimes difficult to report the same information over and over again when you're trying to rest and recuperate. Bill recorded a new message on our telephone answering machine every evening. He reported the events of the day, an update on my condition and thanked callers for their love and concern. He invited people to leave messages so I'd know who called, etc. I remember how thankful I was for their messages and everyone responded very positively to this temporary system of communication.

Allow the evidence of His presence to minister to you. Let His strength be yours. Especially during those times when you feel anything but strong, remember that He is with you BODY, SPIRIT and SOUL (your mind, will and emotions.) So let Him heal your body, let His Spirit comfort you and turn your mind, will and emotions to Him as He cares for you.

Another Tip or Two

I wish there were "tips" that would GUARANTEE you won't get breast cancer, but thankfully research and studies show that making some lifestyle changes may lessen your risk.

I'm sure you've heard these before, but I urge you to:

Not Smoke. While smoking may not cause breast cancer per se, it can increase the chance of blood clots, heart disease and other cancers.

Maintain a healthy weight and regular exercise routine. Your risk of getting breast cancer may decrease because excess fat may stimulate excess estrogen production, which has been linked to breast cancer. Plus, regular exercise reduces stress. Find something FUN, some type of exercise that you ENJOY doing. This will also give you something to look forward to every day.

Modify your diet. Try to decrease your caffeine intake. Try to decrease your daily fat intake, especially saturated fats or hydrogenated fats. Eat leaner meats and cut down on the amount of red meat you consume. Use "good" fats such as olive oil or canola oil. Increase your fiber intake by eating whole grains, fresh vegetables and fruit. Fresh fruit and vegetables also have antioxidant properties and micro nutrients that may actually prevent cancer.

Recipes

I've included the recipes for a few of the wonderful treats that were delivered to my family after my surgeries. Perhaps you'd like to prepare them and share them with someone you know.

Enjoy!

Fresh Apple Muffins

2 Cups flour
2 tsp. cinnamon
1 tsp. baking soda
½ tsp. salt
2 eggs
1 Cup oil
1 Cup sugar
1 tsp. vanilla
4 Cups peeled, chopped Granny Smith apples
1 Cup chopped walnuts

In a small bowl, stir together flour, cinnamon, baking soda and salt; set aside. In a large bowl beat eggs until foamy; beat in oil, sugar and vanilla. Stir in flour mixture until blended; stir in apples and nuts.

Spoon into cupcake tin lined with paper cupcake/muffin cups. Bake at 350 degrees for 20 minutes or until toothpick inserted comes out clean. Yield: 24 muffins.

Bran Muffins

3 ¾ Cups oat bran
2 Cups whole wheat flour
1/3 Cup brown sugar
¾ tsp. salt
1 Tbs. baking soda
1 ½ Cups raisins
3 eggs, beaten
1 ½ Cups buttermilk
¾ Cup oil
½ Cup molasses
½ Cup honey

Combine dry ingredients in large bowl. Combine wet
ingredients. Add the wet ingredients to the dry and stir
until blended well. Add raisins. (Mixture will be very
moist.)

Spoon batter into paper-lined muffin tin.
Bake at 425 degrees for 15 minutes.
(These also freeze well.)

Mandarin Orange Lettuce Salad

Fresh Romaine lettuce
1 Can Mandarin oranges, drained
Slivered almonds

Dressing:

¼ Cup oil
2 Tbs. vinegar
2 Tbs. sugar
1 Tbs. fresh parsley, minced
1 tsp. salt
Dash pepper

Tear lettuce into bite-sized pieces. Add oranges.
Coat almonds with approximately 3 tsp. sugar and
toast in a frying pan until crisp. Cool toasted almonds
and add to salad mixture. Pour dressing over salad,
toss and serve.

Note: If delivering this salad to a friend, bring dressing
in separate container so it can be added just before
serving.

Crunchy Marinated Vegetable Salad

1 can whole kernel corn, drained
1 can water chestnuts, drained and chopped
1 can dark red kidney beans, rinsed and drained
1 can light red kidney beans, rinsed and drained
1 package frozen peas, rinsed and drained
1 onion, finely chopped
1 green pepper, finely chopped

Marinade:

1 cup sugar
½ cup vinegar
¾ cup oil

Heat sugar and vinegar to boil, simmering until sugar is completely dissolved. Add oil. Cool completely.

Mix vegetables in large bowl. Add cooled marinade and toss well.

Refrigerate overnight in a sealed container.

Vegetable Medley

1 Can red kidney beans, drained
1 Can garbanzo beans, drained
1 Large SWEET Red Pepper, chopped
1 Large green pepper, chopped
4 Large celery stalks, chopped
2 Large fresh tomatoes, quartered
1 Large onion, sliced
3 Tbs. oil
1 clove garlic
1 tsp. paprika
Canned vegetable juice

Place all ingredients (except tomatoes) into casserole dish. Cover and bake at 350 degrees for 15 minutes. Add tomatoes and cook until warm and bubbly.

Applesauce

5-6 fresh apples, peeled or unpeeled
½ Cup water
¼ Cup brown sugar
¼ tsp. cinnamon
1/8 tsp. nutmeg

Core and quarter apples. Simmer in water for 5-10 minutes, stirring occasionally. Stir in remaining ingredients and simmer 1 minute. Process in blender until desired consistency.

Note: This also freezes well.

Chicken (or Turkey) Soup

Bring to a boil and simmer, covered, for five minutes:

8 Cups water
Soup Mix*
1 Carrot, diced

Then stir in 3 Cups diced chicken (or turkey)
and simmer for five minutes more.

* Soup Mix:

1 Cup (or more) noodles
1 Tbs. onion, minced
2 ½ Tbs. bouillon granules
1 ½ tsp. pepper
¼ tsp. thyme
1/8 tsp. celery seed
1/8 tsp. garlic
1 large bay leaf (discard before serving)

Hearty Bean Soup

1 large onion, minced
1 bunch fresh baby spinach, washed
1 jar salsa
1 can whole kernel corn
1 can fat-free refried beans
1 can stewed tomatoes
1 can fat-free vegetable broth
1 can navy beans, drained
1 can red kidney beans, drained
1 can garbanzo beans, drained

Sauté onion in a bit of olive oil until tender.
Add the salsa and canned ingredients.
Simmer until hot and bubbly.
Add fresh spinach and simmer until wilted.
Garnish with freshly grated cheddar cheese, if desired.

Family Chicken

5 boneless, skinless chicken breasts
2 Cans low-fat beef broth
4 Tbs. fresh lemon juice
3 Tbs. olive oil
3 Tbs. corn starch
3 Tbs. ice-cold water

Sauté chicken in oil in large Dutch oven until golden brown and cooked. Poor beef broth and lemon juice over chicken. Cover and simmer for 20 minutes. Mix cornstarch into ice water and stir until well blended. Stir cornstarch mixture into hot chicken mixture. Cook for five minutes or until sauce is thickened.

Serve with brown rice, fresh fruit salad and pita bread.

Chicken Crescent Almandine

3 Cups chicken, cooked and cubed
1 Can 98% fat free cream of mushroom soup
1 Cup sliced water chestnuts, drained
½ Cup chopped mushrooms, drained
2/3 Cup low-fat mayonnaise
½ Cup celery, chopped
½ Cup onions, chopped
½ Cup low-fat sour cream

1 8 oz. can crescent rolls
2/3 Cup low-fat Swiss cheese, shredded
½ Cup slivered almonds
2-4 Tbs. butter, melted

Preheat oven to 375 degrees. In a large saucepan
combine the first 8 ingredients. Cook over medium heat
until mixture is hot and bubbly. Pour into greased 9x13
baking dish. Separate crescent rolls into 2 rectangles.
Place rectangles over hot chicken mixture. Combine
remaining ingredients and spread over the dough.
Bake 20-25 minutes until the crust is golden brown.

Carole's Quick Chuck Roast

4 lb. chuck roast
1 oz. bottle steak sauce
1 package dry onion soup mix
1 can 98% fat-free cream of mushroom soup

Remove all visible fat and place roast onto a LARGE sheet of aluminum foil. Pierce roast all over with a fork. Pour the entire bottle of steak sauce over the roast being careful to keep the sauce on the meat/foil. Pour dry onion soup mix over meat and using a spatula combine soup mix with steak sauce to form a "paste" on the roast. Next "frost" the roast with the cream of mushroom soup. (Note: This will not LOOK particularly appetizing at this stage, but trust me, it will taste great!)

Wrap the roast completely in the aluminum foil. Use several additional sheets if necessary. (This keeps the gravy from escaping.) Place the foil-wrapped meat in a roasting pan and cook at 350 degrees for three hours. Remove from the oven and, still wrapped, allow the meat to "rest" for thirty minutes before serving.

Note: This is the same recipe as found in Chapter 19.
For your convenience, I've also included it here.

Microwave Elephant Stew

1 Medium-sized Elephant
Salt and Pepper to taste
2 Rabbits (optional)

Cut elephant into bite-sized pieces. This should take
about 2 months. Add enough brown gravy to cover
meat. Insert temperature probe. Cook in microwave
on high for about four weeks or until tender. Taste for
seasonings. This will serve about 3,000 hungry people.
If more are expected, 2 rabbits may be added, but only
if necessary, as many people do not like to find a hare in
their stew!

(I told you, laughter is some of the best medicine!) ☺

There's Nothing Like the Truth

Caring and devoted doctors and nurses, significant research breakthroughs, exciting new studies and compelling testimonials from cancer survivors are all wonderful sources of strength and hope. But there's NOTHING as powerful as the TRUTH presented in God's Word.

Here are some promises from The Bible, God's Word. Receive them as a soothing balm for your weary soul. Let God encourage you and minister to you as ONLY He can:

"This is my comfort in my affliction, for Your Word has given me life." (Psalm 119:50[NKJV])

"I will never forget Your precepts, for by them You have given me life." (Psalm 119:93[NKJV])

"Every word of God is pure; He is a shield to those who put their trust in Him." (Proverbs 30:5[NKJV])

"My son (daughter), give attention to My words; incline your ear to My sayings. Do not let them depart from your eyes; keep them in the midst of your heart; For they are life to those who find them, and health to all their flesh." (Proverbs 4:20-22[NKJV])

"So then faith comes by hearing, and hearing by the Word of God." (Romans 10:17^{NKJV})

"As for God, His way is perfect; the Word of the Lord is proven; He is a shield to all who trust in Him." (Psalm 18:30^{NKJV})

"Let us hold fast the confession of our hope without wavering, for He who promised is faithful." (Hebrews 10:23^{NKJV})

"Be of good courage, and He shall strengthen your heart, all you who hope in the Lord." (Psalm 31:24^{NKJV})

"For the eyes of the Lord are on the righteous, and His ears are open to their prayers..." (1 Peter 3:12a^{NKJV})

"For the Father, Himself, loves you, because you have loved Me, and have believed that I came forth from God." (John 16:27^{NKJV})

"Peace I leave with you. My peace I give to you; not as the world gives do I give to you. Let not your heart be troubled, neither let it be afraid." (John 14:27^{NKJV})

"Trust in the Lord with all your heart, and lean not on your own understanding; in all your ways acknowledge Him, and He shall direct your paths." (Proverbs 3:5-6^{NKJV})

"My soul, wait silently for God alone, for my expectation is from Him." (Psalm 62:5^{NKJV})

"For I am confident of this very thing, that He Who began a good work in you will complete it until the day of Christ Jesus." (Philippians 1:6^{NKJV})

"The Lord will strengthen him (her) on his (her) bed of illness…" (Psalm 41:3^{NKJV})

"The Lord is good, a strong hold in the day of trouble; and He knoweth them that trust in Him." (Nahum 1:7^{KJV})

"Let us therefore come boldly to the throne of grace, that we may obtain mercy and find grace to help in time of need." (Hebrews 4:16^{NKJV})

"And those who know Your name will put their trust in You; for You, Lord, have not forsaken those who seek You." (Psalm 9:10^{NKJV})

"Heal me, O Lord, and I shall be healed; save me, and I shall be saved, for You are my praise." (Jeremiah 17:14^{KJV})

"O Lord my God, I cried out to You, and You healed me." (Psalm 30:2^{NKJV})

"…and lo, I am with you always, even to the end of the age." (Matthew 28:20b^{NASB})

"And we know that God causes all things to work together for good to those who love God, to those who are called according to His purpose." (Romans 8:28^{NASB})

"Finally, brethren, whatever is true, whatever is honorable, whatever is right, whatever is pure, whatever is lovely, whatever is of good repute, if there is any excellence and if anything worthy of praise, let your mind dwell on these things. The things you have learned and received and heard and seen in Me, practice these things; and the God of peace shall be with you." (Philippians 4:8-9[NASB])

"Eye has not seen, nor ear heard, nor have entered into the heart of man the things which God has prepared for those who love Him." (1 Corinthians 2:9[NKJV])

❦❋❧

*"Now may the
God of hope
fill you with all
joy and peace in
believing, that you
may abound in hope
by the power of the
Holy Spirit."*

(Romans 15:13[NASB])

Notes

Notes

Printed in the United States
93739LV00005B/271-309/A